MAKING MODERNISM SOVIET

MAKING MODERNISM SOVIET

The Russian Avant-Garde in the Early Soviet Era, 1918–1928

Pamela Kachurin

NORTHWESTERN UNIVERSITY PRESS
EVANSTON, ILLINOIS

Northwestern University Press
www.nupress.northwestern.edu

This book has been published with the support of the Andrew W. Mellon Foundation.

Printed in the United States of America

ISBN 978-0-8101-3130-9

The Library of Congress has cataloged the original, hardcover edition as follows:

Kachurin, Pamela Jill.
Making modernism Soviet: the Russian avant-garde in the early Soviet era, 1918–1928 / Pamela Kachurin.
p. cm.
Substantially revised version of the author's thesis (1998).
Includes bibliographical references and index.
ISBN 978-0-8101-2928-3 (cloth : alk. paper)
1. Art, Soviet. 2. Modernism (Art)—Soviet Union. 3. Avant-garde (Aesthetics)—Soviet Union. 4. Art—Political aspects—Soviet Union. 5. Artists and museums—Soviet Union—History—20th century. I. Title.
N6988.5.M64K33 2013
709.470904—dc23

2013002282

For my father, Leon Edward Kachurin (1926–2007)

Contents

Illustrations

Tables

Acknowledgments

This book is a substantially revised version of my doctoral dissertation, completed in 1998. My appraisal of the relationship between the modern artists under consideration in this book and the increasingly repressive "state" apparatus has evolved considerably. While the dissertation adopts a "top-down" narrative—wherein the Soviet state and Communist Party actively marginalized modernist artists, causing a "retreat of the avant-garde" in the early Soviet era—this book presents the same artists as significantly more empowered, having developed strategies to not only survive but also thrive in the new Soviet context.

I am grateful to the International Research and Exchanges Board (IREX), the Malevich Foundation, and the Paul Mellon Foundation for supporting the process of revision and the resulting book. The editorial staff of Northwestern University Press, specifically Michael Levine and Sara Dreyfuss, deserve mention as well.

I would like to acknowledge the following colleagues and friends who have supported me and my work over the years: Edna Andrews, Carol Apollonio, Rosalind Blakesley, Michael David-Fox, Mara Deutsch, Charlotte Douglas, Lee Farrow, Vicki Gabriner, Jehanne Gheith, Mary Giles, Musya Glants, Nina Gurianova, Sona Hoisington, Beth Holmgren, Karen Kettering, Sumi and Ilmee Kim, Christine Kondoleon, Robert Krikorian, Patricia Leighten, Christina Lodder, Paola Martino, Genna Miller, Jennifer Minnelli, Paul Mitchinson, Susan Reid, Alla Rosenfeld, Rochelle Ruthchild, Terri Sabatos, Esty Schachter, Jane Sharp, Mindy Spadacenta, Kristine Stiles, Nina Tumarkin, Erika Wolf, and with special thanks to Janet Kennedy for all your wisdom, wit, and kindness.

I would like to thank my family—Penny Kachurin, the Weisses, Lora and Alex Zitser, the Weingers, and the Weiners—for their love and support. Hailey, you are the light of my life. Words are insufficient to express my gratitude to Erik Zitser—husband, friend, editor, and Slavic bibliographer extraordinaire—who made this book possible.

Abbreviations

AKhRR: Association of Artists of Revolutionary Russia, 1922–32

GAKhN: State Academy of Artistic Research. Operated within Glavnauka 1921–31

GIII: State Institute of the History of Art. Operated within Leningrad branch of Glavnauka 1921–31

GINKhUK: State Institute of Artistic Culture, formerly Museum of Artistic Culture. Operated within the Art Department of Glavnauka 1924–26

Glaviskusstvo: Main Arts Administration. Operated within Narkompros 1927–31

Glavkhudkom: Main Arts Committee. Operated within the Academic Center within Narkompros 1921–22

Glavmuzei: Main Museum Administration; formerly Department of Preservation. Operated within Glavnauka 1921–27

Glavnauka: Main Administration of Scientific and Scientific-Artistic Institutes. Operated within Narkompros 1922–33

Glavpolitprosvet: Main Administration of Political Education. Operated within Narkompros 1920–30

Glavprofobr: Main Administration of Professional Education. Operated within Narkompros 1920–30

Glavsotsvos: Main Administration of Social Training. Operated within Narkompros 1920–30

Gubprofobr: Regional Administration of Professional Education. Operated under Glavprofobr 1920–30

Ispolkom: Executive Committee within any legislative body

IZO: Department of Fine Arts. Operated within Narkompros 1918–21

Narkompros: People's Commissariat of Enlightenment 1917–31

NEP: New Economic Policy 1921–28

OKhOBR: Department of Art Education. Functioned within Glavprofobr 1921–27

OST: Society of Easel Painters 1922–32

RABIS: Art Workers' Union (Artists' Trade Union) 1919–24

Sovnarkom: Council of People's Commissars, highest administrative body in the state apparatus

SVOMAS: Free Art Studios. Operated under IZO Narkompros 1918–20

UNOVIS: Supporters of the New Art. Operated in Vitebsk 1920–22

VKhUTEMAS: Higher Artistic-Technical Studios, replaced SVOMAS, 1920

VSNKh: All-Union Council on the National Economy

VUZ: Higher Academic Institute/College. Operated within Glavprofobr

Introduction

During the first quarter of the twentieth century, at the very start of the Soviet experiment in social engineering and cultural revolution, many members of Russia's historic "avant-garde"—Kazimir Malevich, Vladimir Tatlin, Natan Al'tman, David Shterenberg, Alexander Rodchenko, and Vassily Kandinsky—went to work for the Bolsheviks, finding gainful employment as museum directors, art school teachers, and arts administrators. Yet until now, neither the extent of these modernists' involvement in the nascent Soviet cultural apparatus nor the effect of this involvement on their political and artistic identities has ever been fully analyzed. By describing the symbiotic relationship between modernist artists and the Bolshevik state, this study seeks not only to provide a new perspective on the political and professional careers of some of the most important figures of the Russian avant-garde but also to contribute to a growing literature about European modernists' engagement with twentieth-century political ideologies like Fascism and Communism.[1]

Echoing Paul Wood's critique of much of the extant scholarship about the Russian avant-garde, this book argues that previous attempts to disassociate Russian modernists from the revolutionary aspirations of the Bolsheviks by depicting them as "political virgins," idealistic innocents, or helpless victims have only hindered historical investigations into the political, and specifically Communist, potential of avant-garde artistic production.[2] As we will see, most Russian modernists were not content to play the role of innocent martyrs. Both as artists and as administrators, they actively participated in the Soviet project, directly engaging with Bolshevism to realize their own creative visions of aesthetic and social transformation under the aegis of state patronage. Using their positions within the expanding Soviet arts bureaucracy to build up networks of like-minded colleagues, Russian modernists were able to survive and even thrive during a time of tremendous political upheaval and economic chaos. Along the way, individual members of the Russian avant-garde not only produced some of their most important works of art, but also contributed to the centralization and standardization of the Soviet art world—a "sovietization" of culture that mirrored the processes taking place in the spheres of literature, theater, and intellectual life in general.[3]

As Soviet functionaries, Russian modernist artists incorporated Bolshevik rhetoric into their creative and administrative work and actively participated in the development of socialist culture. In fact, most Russian visual artists, regardless of their political sympathies, participated in what Stephen Kotkin and other historians of early Soviet Russia have dubbed Bolshevik "self-fashioning."[4] Like other Soviet citizens, individual modernist artists performed a "state-sponsored game of social identities" in which the line between "true believers" and those just playing the game became blurred, and "speaking Bolshevik" became the only and "necessary mode of participation."[5] Russia's modernists also played a vital role in the nascent Soviet state's public culture, in which "speaking Bolshevik" was mandatory. Although Russia's modernists had played a role in public culture before 1917,[6] the patronage that they received under the new regime allowed them to move from the margins of the art world to its very center, most visibly, for example, by carrying out commissions to decorate the major cities for early Bolshevik festivals.[7] Adopting the language of Bolshevism to describe their own projects, as well as the programs of the institutions with which they were affiliated, thus not only allowed modernist artists to secure financial and ideological support from the Soviet state, but also demonstrated the artists' continued commitment to active participation in the evolving discourse of Soviet life. In other words, I lay to rest the myth of a one-way imposition of control from above, and discuss the great extent to which there was a dynamic relationship between the power brokers and cultural institutions.[8] While we may never know the extent to which individual modernists internalized Bolshevik rhetoric, this book clearly demonstrates the commitment of many leading figures of the Russian avant-garde to the task of creating a socially transformative visual language, appropriate for the new Soviet context.

Each one of the following three chapters analyzes a different Soviet art institution, tracing its evolution from the October Revolution (1917) through the period of post–Civil War reconstruction known in Soviet historiography as the "New Economic Policy" or "NEP" (1921–28).[9] The latter period has been associated with a liberal cultural policy and corresponding artistic freedom that have traditionally been used to explain—and to justify—the modernists' decision to work for the Soviet state. But as the interlinked examples that make up the narrative of this book demonstrate, the NEP period was actually characterized instead by restrictive measures aimed at curtailing, circumscribing, and ultimately controlling all activities in the sphere of the visual arts—measures that were implemented, and in some cases initiated, not by faceless Soviet bureaucrats, but by the modernist artists in the Soviet art institutions under study. This view contests the myth of Russia's modernists as "innocent children" who, upon attempting to realize their own utopian visions, were "stopped in their tracks" and crushed by Soviet power.[10] It also challenges the validity of the very conception that the Leninist 1920s and the Stalinist 1930s were fundamentally distinct periods of Soviet cultural policy.[11] In that sense, my analysis of Soviet art institutions, and the behavior of modernists within them, corroborates and builds upon the work that scholars like Katerina Clark, Michael David-Fox, Sheila Fitzpatrick, and Stuart Finkel have been doing on other cultural institutions and cultural processes in the early Soviet era.[12]

Although focusing on a different institution, each chapter in this book emphasizes the central role that networks played in the founding and survival of art institutions and the individuals therein. As any student of Russian modernism knows, there was a bewildering number of art groupings in the late imperial period, and affiliations with such groups could last as long as twenty years (as is the case, for example, with the core of the "World of Art" network) or as short as one exhibition (for example, the Donkey's Tail). The self-identification of artists with particular groups continued into the Soviet period, and provided the foundation for building relationships of trust among a small coterie of colleagues, who depended on one another and did their best to protect one another from the hardships and vagaries of life in the first Communist country. They did so by relying not only on one another, however, but also on the patronage of one or two highly placed Bolshevik officials. As Sheila Fitzpatrick has observed:

> The feature that distinguished Soviet patronage from other varieties was that the state was the monopoly distributor in a context of shortages of all goods and services. State monopoly meant that allocation was a major function of the Soviet bureaucracy . . . The ultimate allocational decisions were made by bureaucrats—but on personalistic, not bureaucratic-legal reasons.[13]

For our purposes, it is important to emphasize the key role of Anatoly Lunacharsky (1875–1933), the Bolshevik commissar of enlightenment, who immediately after the 1917 Revolution personally chose individual artists he had known in prewar Paris for administrative posts, including such epigones of modernism as Marc Chagall, David Shterenberg, and Natan Al'tman. As we will see, these strategically placed individuals then formed the nodes of extended networks, which over time evolved into sustained, long-term relationships with other patrons, brokers, and clients, who were within a handful of key institutions.[14] For the modernists who worked within the Soviet arts administration, these institutions were the

People's Commissariat of Enlightenment, and the museums and institutes that constitute the subject of each of the three chapters. Unlike prerevolutionary "circles" (*kruzhki*), which were often sites of resistance to the imperial regime, the newly formed networks in the early Soviet era, in both the literary and the artistic world, were profoundly pragmatic, and part of the fabric of Soviet officialdom.[15] So much so, in fact, that terms like "family circle" or "nest" became a standard element of the Soviet political vocabulary, most frequently as epithets to denounce various forms of "abuse" and "corruption" within the state and party apparatus. That is why throughout this study I will generally use the more neutral word "network" or "circle" to characterize such unofficial forms of local self-organization among modernists both within and outside of the Soviet art administration. In this way I hope to remove some of the moral opprobrium from a common political practice that was as much a means of collective survival as of collective self-advancement.[16]

The variety and sheer number of terms to describe the artists associated with Russian modernism—"avant-garde," "futurists," "leftists," and "formalists"—also requires some explication. After the October Revolution, these epithets were used interchangeably in Soviet art criticism to describe the group of artists, writers, and theorists associated with modernist trends. However, the great majority of artists grouped under the term "futurist" had little to do with the "Futurist" group that thrived between 1911 and 1917.[17] And the well-worn term "avant-garde" was applied to the Russian modernists in retrospect.[18] That is why this monograph primarily will use the more general terms "modernist" and "vanguard" instead of "Futurist," "avant-gardist," or "leftist" artist, except in quotations from the press and officials in the Soviet cultural bureaucracy, who employed these terms, again, almost exclusively in a disparaging way.[19] Of course, "modernism" itself is an overburdened concept. For the purposes of this study, I will define "modernist art" as any work of art that employs a particular range of themes (including, for example, modern and urban life, industrialization, politicized discourses, technology) and visual strategies (for example, primitivism, fragmentation, abstraction, collage, use of nonart materials) to engage with the condition of modernity by using an openly subjective visual language that invites multiple interpretations. This admittedly broad definition seeks to capture the very variety that characterized this truly global art movement, which transcended contemporary national borders and political affiliations, and flourished from the second half of the nineteenth until the end of the twentieth centuries.

The first chapter of this study provides the first comprehensive "behind the scenes" history of the Moscow Museum of Painterly Culture, a unique Soviet art institution which was intended as a repository for the work of all living Russian artists, but which ultimately became the de facto home to painters devoted to modernist experimentation within a socialist context.[20] Chapter One traces the museum's foundations from the earliest days of Bolshevik authority to the very end of 1928, relying on decrees relevant to all Moscow museums to contextualize the archivally based study of this particular modernist preserve. The narrative describes Kandinsky's and Rodchenko's ideologically motivated efforts to reshape this innovative institution into a museum more suitable for the tastes of a broader, "proletarian" audience; and then details the struggles of its directors—first Rodchenko, then another modernist, Pyotr Vil'yams—to keep the museum operational in the context of dwindling economic and ideological support. I argue that to remain open during the financial crises wrought by years of war and revolution, the state-funded museum began to operate according to the principles articulated by the designers of the New Economic Policy, trying to draw in paying customers by offering programs of a more popular character. In the process, Rodchenko and his successor managed to create a novel type of museum, in which modernist art was tied to the very development of the socialist state.

Chapter Two builds upon the extant and copious scholarship on Malevich's activities in Vitebsk by providing a detailed treatment of how the school in which the founder of Suprematism was employed functioned in the context of governmental demands that all educational institutions serve as ideological training grounds.[21] Central to this chapter is a discussion of how the local cultural apparatus and art school administration interpreted and implemented decrees issuing from Moscow, as well as the great extent to which, despite geographic distance, Vitebsk participated in the processes of consolidation and centralization that were occurring in the Soviet capital. Malevich's artistic, theoretical, and pedagogical activities at the Vitebsk School of Art have been explicated elsewhere; what has not been examined, and what this chapter hopes to provide, is a discussion of the way that Vera Ermolaeva (another modernist artist and Chagall's successor as director) kept the school open, funded, and sympathetic to the kind of artistic experimentation demonstrated by Malevich and his students. Through examination of local decrees about art institutes and Ermolaeva's documentation of school activities, I demonstrate that the female art school director's bureaucratic savvy (which included adjusting the curriculum to incorporate training in Marxism-Leninism, as well as practical skills such as carpentry) enabled this nest of modernism to survive at a time when nearly half of all cultural institutions were shut down. This chapter also describes in depth how the well-known art group "Supporters of the

New Art" (UNOVIS), led by Kazimir Malevich and El Lissitzky, flourished within the prevailing atmosphere of hostility toward the intelligentsia among the Bolshevik leadership. From this perspective, UNOVIS's innovative "production"-oriented program (which was to be carried out by a "collective" rather than an individual) was part of the modernist artists' efforts to demonstrate that they, too, were able to promote "proletarian values." This chapter presents the UNOVIS group as a network of individuals, led by Malevich, whose modernist project of creating a parallel "party" succeeded in making Suprematism Soviet.

The third and final chapter provides a detailed examination of how the Petrograd Museum of Artistic Culture, and its successor, the State Institute of Artistic Culture (GINKhUK), managed not only to survive, but also to thrive as a haven for artistic and theoretical innovation into the late 1920s, a period which saw dramatically increased control over the creative sphere and that culminated in the imposition of Stalinist orthodoxy.[22] In the wake of the expulsion of over 200 members of the intelligentsia from the Russian Soviet Federative Socialist Republic, Malevich and his network of colleagues transformed the identity of the Museum of Artistic Culture from one devoted primarily to public display to a Soviet research institute—complete with laboratories. As an exemplary Soviet institution devoted to modernist experimentation and exhibition, the museum and its successor institute also provided space and resources for Malevich to elaborate his Marxist-inflected pedagogical system "On the Additional Element in Art." I argue that this was only possible thanks to the directors' (first Andrii Taran's and then Malevich's) ability to carve out an independent identity (and budget) for this institution, as well as their knack for creating a close-knit circle that maintained a united front against governmental interference and, if necessary, evicted those artists (like Tatlin) whose behavior threatened the group as a whole.

In sum, this study of the sovietization of Russian modernism argues that "the avant-garde" and "the state" should not be viewed as distinct entities struggling against each other. The term "avant-garde" subsumes at least as many personal, political, professional, and generational differences as the "working class" or the "intelligentsia." Similarly, "the state," even the supposedly totalitarian variety, was not some kind of unitary, unchanging, bureaucratic apparatus intent on brutally repressing modernist art production and crushing individuals at will. In practice, "the state" was actually composed of interlocking networks of individuals, who played the role of brokers and patrons, and who either supported their clients in the art community or withdrew that support, depending on which way the political winds were blowing at a particular moment. The book depicts Russian modernists as political actors, strategically situated in key art institutions and actively engaged with Marxist ideology within an increasingly repressive Soviet state. It also demonstrates that patronage patterns began to shift long before the imposition of "Socialist Realism" under Joseph Stalin and that already during the New Economic Policy opposing voices sought to curtail the modernist artists' role in creating Bolshevik "civic society" (*obshchestvennost'*) and limit, if not eliminate, modernist artists' opportunities to participate in the evolving discourse of Soviet life. What this book does not do is offer an exhaustive study of Russian modernism: since my focus is on networks and individuals operating within institutions, there is far more to be said on the art of this period itself. Luckily, there is an abundance of work devoted to this topic.[23] Indeed, this book could not have been written without the pioneering and expertly researched work of Elena Basner, John Bowlt, Timothy Clark, Charlotte Douglas, Tatiana Goriacheva, Maria Gough, Boris Groys, Nina Gurianova, Irina Karasik, Christina Kiaer, Christina Lodder, E. N. Petrova, Jane Sharp, Aleksandra Shatskikh, Larissa Zhadova, and a host of other scholars, whose focus on modernist visual practice and its theoretical underpinning provides the foundation on which this social and institutional history is built.

MAKING MODERNISM SOVIET

Chapter One

The Great Experiment:
The Moscow Museum of Painterly Culture, 1918–1928

This chapter provides the first comprehensive, archive-based history of the Moscow Museum of Painterly Culture (Muzei zhivopisnoi kul'tury, hereafter, MZhK)—a unique Soviet institution that was created in 1918 as a repository for the work of all living Russian artists, but that quickly became the de facto home to artists devoted to modernist experimentation within a socialist context.[1] This chapter traces the Museum of Painterly Culture's turbulent ten-year existence, from the earliest days of Bolshevik authority to the very end of the NEP period in 1928. It chronicles the efforts of four successive directors—Vassily Kandinsky (1866–1944), Alexander Rodchenko (1891–1956), Pyotr Vil'yams (1902–1947), and Lazar Vainer (1885–1933)—to keep the museum operational in the context of dwindling economic and ideological support. More controversially, it also demonstrates the high level of engagement on the part of the museum's staff with the ideals of Bolshevism—an engagement that was proactive rather than reactive, and that came to define both the contours of the Moscow Museum of Painterly Culture and the artistic production of the artists associated with it. As we will see, to remain open during the financial crises and bureaucratic reorganizations wrought by the designers of the New Economic Policy, the state-funded museum began to operate in a more commercial mode, trying to draw in paying customers by offering programs suitable for the tastes of a broader "proletarian" audience. This attempt to reshape a modernist preserve into a popular museum hinged on its directors' abilities to create an appropriately socialist context for modernist experimentation, as well as to sell that creation to their patrons within the Soviet art administration.

Narkompros's Department of Fine Arts and the Genesis of the Museum of Painterly Culture

Because the new Bolshevik leadership considered the education and ideological training of the country's population as the key to both the short- and long-term survival of Soviet authority, one of their first acts was the creation of the People's Commissariat of Enlightenment (Narodny kommissariat prosveshcheniya; hereafter, Narkompros). This state organ was formed in November 1917 and entrusted with all matters related to the cultural and educational spheres: literature, theater, music, fine arts, publishing, primary and secondary schooling, and professional education. Thanks to the authority and political connections of Anatoly Lunacharsky (1875–1933), a Marxist philosopher and literary critic who served as its first commissar, Narkompros enjoyed a special status within the nascent Soviet bureaucracy, and was funded accordingly.[2] So was its Department of Fine Arts (Otdel izobrazitel'nogo iskusstv; hereafter, IZO), which was created in January 1918 and charged with the overwhelming task of administering the country's art schools, art museums, exhibitions, public art projects, and publications related to the fine arts.[3] To head the Department of Fine Arts, Lunacharsky appointed David Shterenberg (1881–1948)—a modernist painter whom the future commissar of enlightenment had met in Paris in 1915, and whom he had praised for his realism and economical style.[4] Although technically the Department of Fine Arts was responsible directly to Lunacharsky, in practice the head of Narkompros delegated much of the day-to-day responsibilities to Shterenberg and the Department of Fine Arts Collegium, the administrative board charged with dispensing funds, approving all activities and expenditures, and the operation for the entire Department of Fine Arts.

The founding of Narkompros and the Department of Fine Arts created many new opportunities for working artists, especially those who for one reason or another had been marginalized under the Old Regime. Lunacharsky encouraged Narkompros to hire professional artists, who were considered "necessary specialists for the Republic" and, hence, were offered many special benefits, including triple rations, during the extended period of economic and political dislocation that accompanied the Russian Civil War (1918–21).[5] There were other material incentives to entice artists to work for the Bolsheviks: those employed in state art institutions were exempted from paying the "Extraordinary Tax," which was levied in 1918;[6] and were guaranteed "suitable working conditions," including "a studio and a separate room in which to live"—something that was immensely attractive at a time of extreme housing shortages in the cities.[7] The first artists to offer their services to the Bolsheviks were the "Board of Seven," which included, among others, the Russian art scholar and "Futurist" theorist Nikolai Punin (1888–1953).[8] These men were soon followed by other artists, many of whom also identified themselves as "Futurists"—the umbrella term for all artists working in a modernist visual idiom.[9] One of them was Punin's friend, the artist Vladimir Tatlin (1885–1953), who would play a key role in the genesis of the Museum of Painterly Culture, and whose case provides a window into how Russia's modernists functioned within the early Soviet cultural bureaucracy.[10] Although Tatlin's personal political views at this time are unknown, he was in the vanguard of the general artistic migration toward the Soviet arts administration.[11] From spring 1918 to summer 1919, he worked simultaneously in three positions at, and received three separate salaries from, Narkompros. Besides serving as president of the Department of Fine Arts Collegium, Tatlin held a teaching post at the Moscow Free Art Studios, a new art school founded in 1918 from an amalgamation of the Moscow School of Painting, Sculpture, and Architecture with the Stroganov Art School, and administered by the Department of Fine Arts.[12] He also worked as a staff member in a Department of Fine Arts subdepartment devoted to "Art Construction," which was responsible for two important and ongoing public art endeavors: decorations for the mass festivals staged by the Bolsheviks and the "Plan for Monumental Propaganda."

While others may not have stretched themselves quite as thin as Tatlin, within a year of the Bolshevik takeover, artists associated with Russian modernism occupied key positions within the government arts administration, and especially at the Department of Fine Arts, which had become the primary patron and supporter of their activities and artistic production. By July 1918 many of Russia's modernists held positions within the Department of Fine Arts governing board, including such major players of Russian modernism as Pavel Kuznetsov (1878–1968); Ilya Mashkov (1881–1944), a painter who belonged to the Jack of Diamonds group of which Tatlin was a member; the painters Nadezhda Udal'tsova (1886–1961) and Sophia Dymshits-Tolstaya (1886–1963); Robert Fal'k (1886–1958), one of the founders of Jack of Diamonds; Sergei Konenkov (1874–1971), the "Soviet Rodin"; Vassily Kandinksy (1866–1944), the painter and art theorist; and Kazimir Malevich (1879–1935), originator of Suprematism and Tatlin's longtime rival.[13] It was this small group of government-employed modernist artists that came up with the idea for, and quickly proceeded to form, the collection of the Moscow Museum of Painterly Culture.

The genesis of the Moscow Museum of Painterly Culture can be traced back to a joint project formulated by two members of the Department of Fine Arts Collegium: Vladimir Tatlin and Sophia Dymshits-Tolstaya.

Tatlin and Dymshits-Tolstaya proposed that the Soviet state finance the organization of what they dubbed the "Museum of Contemporary Art," a novel type of museum that would serve as a showcase for the "best works of living art,"[14] which would be displayed not only in the capital, but also in newly established provincial branches spread out across Soviet Russia.[15] Tatlin further specified that acquisitions for this museum would be approved only by the Department of Fine Arts Collegium—of which he was the president—and that artists themselves would choose which works they would sell to the State Purchasing Commission, which they themselves administered.[16] In other words, artists, who just a year before were in difficult financial straits, would now be in a position to sell their own works to a generous new patron: the Soviet state. The Collegium immediately approved Tatlin's suggestion, justifying this obvious conflict of interest on the basis that his plan would "enable the proletariat to understand the significance of contemporary art."[17] The Collegium then went ahead and approved the purchase of paintings from living artists, that is, from one another. The first acquisition made by the Department of Fine Arts Purchasing Commission, in September 1918, was of five paintings by Malevich, for 20,000 rubles, the equivalent of his teaching salary for ten months. Next, Tatlin sold three paintings to the Purchasing Commission for 21,000 rubles. By October 17, 1918, a total of sixty-one works had been purchased for 215,000 rubles, all for the still nonexistent Museum of Contemporary Art.[18] The vast majority of works were by artists associated with vanguard and nonobjective trends: Udal'tsova, Rodchenko, Kandinsky, Ol'ga Rozanova (1886–1918), and Anton Pevsner (1886–1962), all of whom worked within the Department of Fine Arts, and all of whom had the active support of Shterenberg. For example, in his budget proposal for the second half of 1918, the head of the Department of Fine Arts justified his request for an additional one million rubles by arguing that in the last ten to fifteen years "contemporary art had not been collected for either private or public collections"; this was why, in his opinion, modernist art warranted special attention and patronage. Shterenberg saw the proposed Museum of Contemporary Art as a method of redressing perceived inequities from the late imperial period, when modernist artists faced hostile critics and minimal patronage. Furthermore, he claimed that the collection of contemporary art would stimulate a younger generation of artists to study and create works of art.[19] Lunacharsky, ever hopeful of encouraging the creation of a new type of art, responded to the latter argument, but only assigned about 300,000 rubles for purchases.[20]

By November 1918, the plans for the museum were made public in two articles in *The Life of Art* (*Zhizn' iskusstva*), one of which listed the artists whose work had been bought for the museum and the sum paid for the works.[21] The publication of these ambitious plans may have incited an unnamed *Pravda* author to object to the fact that the acquisitions were made "not from artists who deserved it" but only from "Futurists, whose future is still very controversial."[22] Those individuals who were more attuned to the "agony of the intelligentsia," however, were even more perceptive and, sometimes, even more blunt. In a 1919 letter, the writer Count Alexei N. Tolstoy, Dymshits-Tolstaya's ex-husband, attacked "the Futurists here [in Moscow]—Mayakovsky, Tatlin, and others," for "creating a lot of fuss in art" to "glorify themselves and sell their products":

> They are now buying paintings and statues for the People's Museums and the first place is given to the feverish smearings of the Futurists. Aside from that, the Bolsheviks have assigned this Tatlin a bulk sum of 500,000 rubles to be used at his own discretion.[23]

By the time this philippic against the "Futurists" appeared in print, however, it was already obsolete. For as early as December 1918, the plans for a Museum of Contemporary Art, as it was originally envisioned, were abandoned for that of another new museum known as the "Museum of Painterly and Plastic Culture." The modernists in the Department of Fine Arts Collegium, on alert that unchecked self-promotion would be noticed, found it prudent to retreat from their original idea of creating a showcase for their own work, in favor of a museum that corresponded more closely to Narkompros's stated goals of displaying art from all trends and periods.

Between December 1918 and February 1919, the Museum of Contemporary Art slowly metamorphosed into the Museum of Painterly and Plastic Culture—a process that made no dent, however, in the operation of the Purchasing Commission, which continued to acquire works of modern art even after the Collegium formally withdrew its support for the Museum of Contemporary Art. The modernists who authored the revised plan—Rodchenko, Kandinsky, and Alexander Drevin (1889–1938), Udal'tsova's husband—still supported the idea of having a place to showcase vanguard art, but they also took into account the most recent museological discussions, as well as Narkompros's policy of neutrality in the sphere of the arts, when they proposed that the new institution should encompass art from all trends and time periods. The plans for the Museum of Painterly Culture were published in two successive issues (11 and 12) of the Department of Fine Arts journal, *Iskusstvo kommuny* (*Art of the Commune*), ahead of the upcoming Museum Conference in Petrograd. Four days before the opening of the conference, the Department of Fine Arts Collegium also passed a "Declaration of the Department of Fine Arts . . . on the Question About

Principles of Museums," which they planned to present at the conference. Amid the typically modernist amalgam of rhetorical slogans ("Artists! Free art of the past from deathly historical pedantism! Artists! The matter of artistic education is your business since you alone are responsible for artistic creation! Artists of the world! The language in which you speak is understandable to all people!"), the authors of the Department of Fine Arts declaration articulated two main desiderata for the new type of museum: first, that this cultural heritage institution be more "tolerant" of works of the past; and second, that collection development in the field of contemporary art be handled by the artists themselves, rather than museum employees, curators, or directors.[24] In other words, while making a slight concession to official Narkompros policy, the modernists on the Department of Fine Arts Collegium attempted to arrogate to themselves the power to determine the fate of vanguard modernism in the Soviet art world, thereby ensuring that they alone would be entrusted with stewarding their art into the Soviet era.

The Museum Conference opened on February 11, 1919, in the Winter Palace in Petrograd. Lunacharsky's opening speech affirmed the significance of museums in Soviet culture and their primary task in establishing connections between Soviet cultural institutions and the masses.[25] The speech was vague, however, on the basic principles of "artistic culture," that is, the ideas on which the Museum of Painterly and Plastic Culture would be based. In fact, although Nikolai Punin did read a speech declaring the need for this new type of museum, the principles of "artistic culture" were published rather than spoken: first in the journal *Izobrazitel'noe iskusstva* (*Fine Art*) and then in the Department of Fine Arts "Guide" (*Spravochnik*). According to these two publications, the term "artistic culture" referred to any type of artistic production that employed "experimental painterly and plastic techniques"—a definition that was almost synonymous with modernist and contemporary art. From this definition flowed the three principles on which the proposed museum would be founded:

> 1) The concept that artistic culture is an objective criterion of artistic value; 2) the concept of artistic culture contains . . . a creative element [since] artistic culture is nothing other than the culture of artistic inventions; 3) by sustained artistic labor, contemporary art schools have been able to reveal many elements of artistic activity and thereby to establish the objective criterion of artistic value as a professional value.[26]

Despite the opacity of this formulation, it is clear that the authors of the two programmatic articles sought to legitimize vanguard art: first, by casting it as having "objective professional value," and, therefore, as something that was worthy of study, display, and acquisition; and second, by asserting that, at its core, vanguard art was about "invention," that is, precisely the kind of novelty and innovation that was found in the modernist works recently purchased by the artists on the Department of Fine Arts Collegium. This lobbying, both in person and in the press, seemed to pay off: when the discussion finally turned to the creation of a Museum of Painterly and Plastic Culture, the conferees agreed that artists themselves should be in charge of purchasing and choosing works of art for the new type of museum.[27] Even Lunacharsky endorsed this idea on the grounds that it objectively showed the "evolution of labor in the area of art."[28] To work out all the logistical details, the conference-goers appointed a six-man "contact group" composed of representatives from both the Museum and Fine Arts departments—the two units within Narkompros that would be most involved in overseeing and carrying out the proposed plan.

In May 1919, just four months after the Museum Conference, representatives from the Museum Department—the realist painter Igor Grabar (1871–1960), Yu. Mashkovtsev (active 1918–1926), M. Muratov (active 1918–1929), and the art critic Abram Efros (1888–1954)—and of the Fine Arts Department—Tatlin and the art theorist and literary critic Osip Brik (1888–1945), met to discuss their charge. Despite the dire economic and material situation in which they met—no fuel for heat, no space for accommodations[29]—these men successfully formulated the acquisition policy for new museums and decided that the Moscow Museum of Painterly and Plastic Culture should be established in selected rooms of the former Shchukin Mansion.[30] They even agreed to place limits on the amounts paid to artists for their work to a maximum of 7,000 rubles and a minimum of 700—a decision that was almost certainly an attempt to address the irresponsible spending on the part of the Purchasing Commission.[31] Finally, the committee drafted an outline of its plan for the new museum and, on May 30, sent it to the Department of Fine Arts Collegium. Unlike previous attempts to create an appropriately Soviet context for modernist art, however, this plan was drawn up by a group of artists that included individuals from outside the circle of Department of Fine Arts modernists. Consequently, whereas the first plan, formulated by Tatlin and Dymshits-Tolstaya, envisioned the Museum of Contemporary Art as a showcase of the "best living art," that is, composed exclusively of contemporary modernist works; and the second plan, written by Rodchenko, Kandinsky, and Drevin, conceded that a Museum of Painterly and Plastic Culture had to include inventive works typical of both modernist and nonmodernist trends; the plan drawn up by the members of the joint departmental "contact committee" emphasized "methods, composition, construction, and texture," in other words, all technical aspects of the task of painting; and not just modernist painting, but the painting "of all times and all people."[32] The latest plan also underlined the educational role of the museum and stressed its accessibility to the masses, a priority that had been reiterated by Lunacharsky at the Museum Conference in February 1919 and proclaimed as public policy by the Communist Party, at its Eighth Congress, one month later.[33] Although, in fact, this version of the museum plan was not substantially different from the one drawn up immediately before the February conference, some members of the Department of Fine Arts Collegium were not pleased with the result. Kazimir Malevich, for one, saw it as "an enormous concession, an enormous step backward, an enormous covenant with yesterday." The contact committee's recommendations, and particularly its decision to create "a museum on the basis of painterly culture," Malevich warned, meant that eventually "all the trends . . . will end up here"—a situation that potentially undermined the original plan for a museum dedicated to modernist experimentation and diluted the modernist presence in the Moscow Museum of Painterly Culture.[34]

The Moscow Museum of Painterly Culture Under Kandinsky

Although there are some questions about its exact opening date, it is generally accepted that the Moscow Museum of Painterly Culture began operating on June 10, 1919, in five rooms of the former Shchukin Mansion. Both the museum (led by Vassily Kandinsky) and the Purchasing Commission were under the management of the newly created Museum Bureau (led by Alexander Drevin). The division of labor between these three units was extremely fungible, which makes it difficult to determine precisely which unit was undertaking which activity. What is clear is that for the first few months after its opening, the primary activity of the Moscow Museum of Painterly Culture and the Museum Bureau was the organization of affiliated branches throughout the length and breadth of Soviet Russia. In practice, this process entailed selecting on average twenty paintings—recently acquired by the Purchasing Commission—to be sent from Moscow to a city in the provinces.[35] During the summer of 1919, for example, paintings were sent to Vitebsk, Astrakhan', Vyatka, Samara, Smolensk, Voronezh, Simbirsk, Orel, Mster, and Nizhny Novgorod.[36] By the end of 1920, museums were also established in Tobol'sk, Yekaterinburg, Vyatka, Penza, Ufa, and Perm.[37] These impressive numbers belied the fact that most of the provincial museums established by the Museum of Painterly Culture and the Museum Bureau during this time of catastrophic shortages and economic dislocation were quite modest, often consisting of fifteen or twenty paintings hanging in the corridors of the local art school.

The rapid expansion of the network of museums meant that there was now a constant demand for art—particularly the art either created by Department of Fine Arts members or commissioned and purchased through their unit. According to archival sources, the majority of the works that were sent to provincial branches of the Museum of Painterly Culture were contemporary modernist works by Malevich, Udal'tsova, Ol'ga Rozanova (1886–1918), Ilya Mashkov, Mikhail Larionov (1881–1964), Natalia Goncharova (1881–1962), Ivan Kliun (1873–1943), and Liubov' Popova (1889–1924). Because of earlier accusations in the press about nepotism regarding art purchases, Shterenberg, the director of the Department of Fine Arts, refused to sell his own works to the Purchasing Commission. But this did not prevent his colleagues, Kandinsky and Drevin, from writing directly to Lunacharsky to ask the head of Narkompros personally "to authorize the Museum Commission to acquire paintings from the artist Shterenberg."[38] The Purchasing Commission's work continued at fever pitch through 1920. At this time, artists regularly received solicitations to send their work "to the Museum Bureau of Department of Fine Arts for examination by the Purchasing Commission."[39] In a shift away from the unstated policy of acquiring only modernist works, the Purchasing Commission now bought works from artists of all trends, including representatives of an older generation that worked in a more representational style, like Lazar Vainer, a Neoclassically trained artist and the future director of the Museum of Painterly Culture; Abram Arkhipov (1862–1930), a former member of the "Wanderers" (Peredvizhniki); Konstantin Korovin (1861–1939), the leading Russian Impressionist painter; Boris Kustodiev (1878–1927), who studied painting in Il'ya Repin's studio at the Imperial Academy of Arts in St. Petersburg; Leonid Pasternak (1862–1945), the Postimpressionist painter and father of the poet and Nobel Prize–winning novelist; Ivan Cheptsov (1874–1950); and Konstantin Yuon (1875–1958), painters and theater-designers associated with the "World of Art"; as well as younger colleagues such as the Ukrainian-Russian modernist artist Kliment Red'ko (1897–1956).[40] Despite the fact that Lunacharsky made a list of only 143 artists whose work could be purchased, and the state imposed price limits, the Purchasing Commission was able to make a substantial number of art purchases.[41] No exact numbers are available for the period between September 1918 and June 1919. However, by November 1919, 21 sculptures and 650 paintings and drawings had been acquired for 1,715,000 rubles.[42] And by 1920, the Purchasing Commission had purchased 106 sculptures and approximately 1,200 paintings and drawings, for a cost of nearly 11 million rubles.[43]

While the Museum Bureau was occupied with distributing and organizing the exhibition of this large cache of mostly modernist art, Vassily Kandinsky and David Shterenberg were busy trying to justify its utility to their superiors within the state bureaucracy, and to their public. For example, in his January 1920 essay on the "Moscow Museum of Painterly Culture," Kandinsky highlighted the "unique value" of his museum's collection of modernist and nonobjective art and polemicized against art critics who suggested that "Futurism and nonobjectivity of all types cannot be the art of the new era, the art of the proletariat."[44] The Museum of Painterly Culture's director could not simply ignore such accusations, especially since they resonated with the views of some high-placed officials in the Soviet arts administration, including Lunacharsky, who was uneasy with purely formal art. But while conceding that "there is no place for work purely and exclusively of formal value," Kandinsky reassured the readers of *Artistic Life* (*Khudozhestvennaya zhizn'*) that the collection under his supervision did, in fact, demonstrate "progress" in two areas of art: invention and technique.[45] This tack was also adopted by Shterenberg, the director of the museum's board, who wrote an article in the Department of Fine Arts Guide stressing the Museum of Painterly Culture's pedagogical agenda. "The educational significance of these museums," Shterenberg affirmed, "is clear."[46] And so, by implication, was their value to Soviet society. These public attempts to explain the uniqueness and educational value of the Museum of Painterly Culture, however, did not convince the opponents of the modernist artists employed by the Department of Fine Arts. In late 1920, for example, a Marxist critic named Viktor Friche railed against the activities of the Museum Bureau in the pages of *Creativity* (*Tvorchestvo*) in terms that were clearly intended to grab the attention of the upper administration of the People's Commissariat of Enlightenment:

> Acquisition of the museum collection has been mostly of Left artists. The idea itself of the creation of the Museum of Painterly Culture arose to create "their" museum of left art . . . This fact requires the attention of the Proletarian State since art in the R.S.F.S.R is really in danger.

Friche concluded his polemic with a call for what he called "transformational realism," a style of new monumental art that would act directly on the soul.[47]

The fact that pointed critiques like those of Friche did not lead to an investigation of members of the Museum Bureau, and that the acquisition of modernist works and the establishment of provincial museums continued virtually uninterrupted for a period of almost two years, did not mean that the people's commissar of enlightenment believed that modernist art was the most effective vehicle to communicate Soviet ideology. Although one cannot rule out the possibility that Lunacharsky was grateful for the existence of a group of energetic artists who were actually carrying out a plan for cultural enlightenment, the Museum Bureau's ability to act more or less autonomously was most likely the result of the commissar's preoccupation with more pressing concerns, such as the fulfillment of Lenin's December 1919 decree on the "liquidation of illiteracy,"[48] as well as the general administrative chaos that characterized Narkompros in the first years of its existence. This administrative chaos, and the ideological discrepancies that arose from it, prompted the Council of People's Commissars (Soviet narodnykh kommissarov, or Sovnarkom), the highest organ of the Soviet state, headed by Lenin, to intervene in the operation of Lunacharsky's bailiwick. In early November 1920, the Sovnarkom and the Central Committee of the People's Commissariat of Enlightenment launched a massive administrative reorganization, citing Narkompros's "lack of practical efficiency . . . and the prevalence of general arguments and abstract slogans." To "combat these defects" the Central Committee of Narkompros mandated that "specialists" (that is, educated professionals such as artists) could still continue to work within Narkompros, but only under "two indispensable conditions": first, that specialists who were not Communists had to work "under the control" of Communists; and second, that Communists alone could determine the programming and curricula.[49] In an attempt to streamline the various departments that proliferated under Narkompros, all units were distributed between six administrative organs. Particularly careful attention was paid to the reorganization of the artistic sector of Narkompros. Alarmed by the fact that "at present, only five of 700 workers in the art sector are communists," the Sovnarkom resolved that it was necessary to increase the number of Communists in leadership positions and reorganize the executive apparatus of the art section (Department of Fine Arts).[50] All art institutions previously united under Department of Fine Arts of Narkompros were thenceforth divided between the Academic Center (Akademicheskii tsentr), the Main Administration of Professional Education (Glavnoe upravlenie professional'nogo obrazovaniya, or Glavprofobr), and the Main Administration of Political Education (Glavnoe upravlenie politicheskogo prosveshcheniya, or Glavpolitprosvet). The Academic Center—a unit whose primary purpose was to unite the political work of Narkompros by a single policy of "militant ideological work"[51]—was put in charge of the Museum Bureau and the Museum of Painterly Culture in Moscow. The Main Administration of Professional Education took over the administration of all art schools and teachers therein.[52] The Department of Fine Arts lecture and exhibitions bureaus were placed under the Main Administration for Political Education (see figure 1). The reorganization

Figure 1. Narkompros Structure After 1921 Reorganization

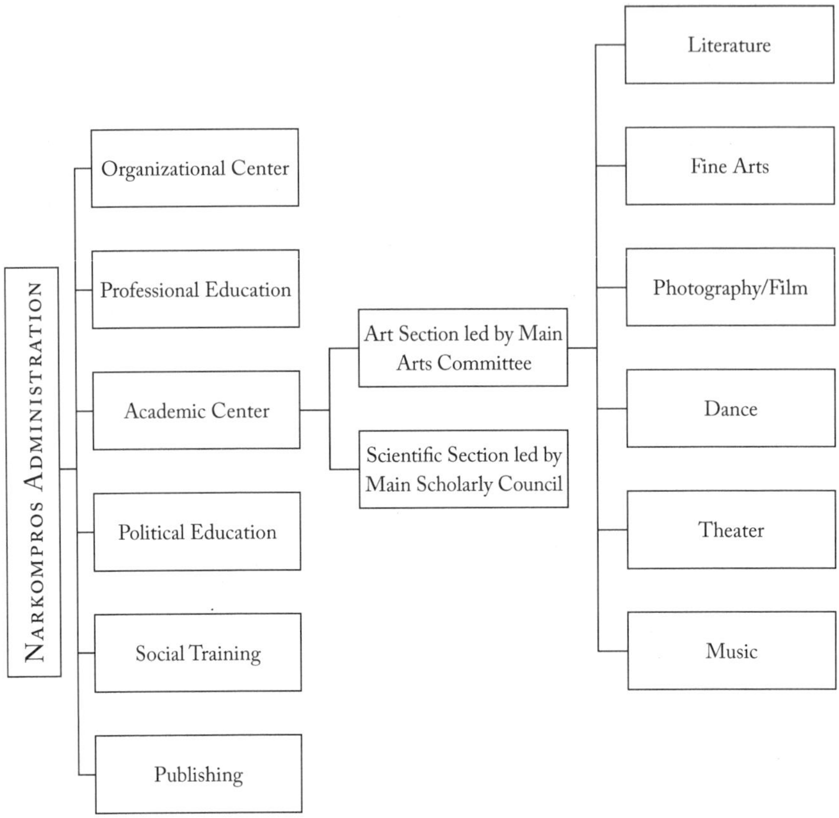

of Narkompros effectively ended the Department of Fine Arts' short-lived monopoly of the arts in Soviet Russia. The process of "sovietization" and centralization had undeniably begun.

The reorganization of Narkompros in 1921 prompted additional anti-Futurist tirades, not least as a way of justifying the new administrative changes. A good example of this is an article by Narkompros official Boris Pliuskin-Kronin about the Main Arts Committee (Glavny khudozhestvenny komitet, or Glavkhudkom), a short-lived institution charged with "work[ing] out the general theoretical direction for all divisions of Narkompros carrying out artistic work and [instituting] observation over them," in an attempt to unify the leadership of the entire artistic life of the republic in agreement with the demands of Marxist Communist ideology.[53] The author of this piece lamented the fact that "for the last three years" the Soviet state had spent "billions on all types of art . . . but the preparation of soil and clearing of the road for new purely proletarian art was not fulfilled." This, he argued, was primarily due to two factors: the "dominance of specialists with false passports [that is, not "real" Soviet citizens] ... who [were] unable [either] to democratize art and use it as an agitational-educational instrument or to pay heed to the art of the proletariat." Pliuskin-Kronin insisted that the "reform" of the art sector—in this case, the Main Arts Committee's assertion of total control over the formulation and financing of all new initiatives—would free individual departments from theoretical planning, so that from now on, they would simply be able to carry out projects.[54] This separation of functions, he averred, would lead "not to the demise, but the new flowering of all types of art."[55] Although the Main Arts Committee's efforts to remove budgetary control from the purview of individual subdepartments ultimately proved ineffectual and counterproductive, the government's decision to move in the direction of increasing centralization over the arts clearly bolstered the courage of the Pliuskin-Kronins in the Soviet art apparatus.

The Moscow Museum of Painterly Culture Under Rodchenko

Despite the more stringent economic and ideological environment at Narkompros, the Moscow Museum of Painterly Culture appeared to operate fairly normally during the first six months of 1921. Alexander Rodchenko, who had been the head of the Museum Bureau since February 1920, took over as the new director of the Museum of Painterly Culture in January 1921, after Kandinsky left for a position at the Russian Academy of Artistic Research. Rodchenko continued his predecessor's policy of supervising the acquisition and distribution of paintings for the network of provincial museums founded by the Museum Bureau, which claimed to have organized thirty-six museum collections throughout Soviet Russia by March 1921.[56] While some "collections" consisted of no more than five paintings, it was still a considerable accomplishment, given the desperately poor working conditions during the last days of the Russian Civil War: no lightbulbs, no paper,[57] and "building[s] where the temperature never averages above 0."[58] Rodchenko also continued Kandinsky's and Shterenberg's efforts to present the Museum of Painterly Culture's collection of vanguard art as the foundation of a well-organized and ideologically correct institution devoted to "artistic-scientific goals, pedagogical goals, and exhibitions." "The Moscow museum," he reported in January 1921, "is a collection of works of all types of fine art: painting, sculpture, spatial forms, graphics, drawings, and handicrafts and architectural projects.... [The provincial museums] are organized under the State Artistic and Production Studios [SVOMAS] for directly serving the pedagogical demands of the studios and are located under the direct management of the Museum Bureau."[59]

But much like his predecessor, the new director of the Museum of Painterly Culture could not placate its critics. Rodchenko's attempt to enact the "militant ideological work" of Narkompros, for example, did not satisfy the young critic and art historian Alexei Alexandrovich Sidorov (1891–1978), the author of a scathing piece about the museum in the January–March 1921 issue of *Creativity.* Sidorov complained that despite the laudable theoretical goals of the museum, during a recent visit to the Museum of Painterly Culture "we saw in front of our eyes the most common survey exhibition of the most extreme painting schools." Except for its leftist bias, the Moscow museum, according to Sidorov, did not have an obvious organizing concept. In fact, Sidorov declared, it was "not a museum but simply [a set of] 'rooms.'" He went on to accuse the organizers of disingenuousness, claiming that the Museum of Painterly Culture "was only an attempt to collect pictures of artists that . . . did not end up in our National Museums" and that "the desire to show themselves [off]" supplanted the "principles of professional-technical matters." Although he continued to consider a "scientific-technical museum of painterly invention and technique as interesting and necessary," Sidorov concluded that "as a museum and as a place for study of 'painterly culture'" the Museum of Painterly Culture "was a failure."[60]

Increasingly, such accusations came to shape the actions of officials at regulatory agencies, including the State Accounting Office, which threatened to close the Moscow Museum of Painterly Culture in May 1921. In response to this unprecedented move, Rodchenko and his wife and collaborator, Varvara Stepanova (1894–1958), wrote an urgent appeal to the State Accounting Office in which they presented their museum as a key Soviet institution, possessing a unique "pedagogical and cultural-educational goal." Rodchenko and Stepanova made sure to point out that "[a] large percentage of visitors are students from the State Art Studios," that is, the Higher Artistic-Technical Studios (Vysshie khudozhestvenno-tekhnicheskie masterskie, hereafter VKhUTEMAS), which were founded in 1920 with the intention "to prepare master artists of the highest qualifications for industry, and builders and managers for professional-technical education."[61] In other words, the Museum of Painterly Culture was central to the economic survival of nascent Soviet Russia and the longer-term construction of socialism. They added: "Also there are excursions from the provinces and foreign visitors."[62] Closing the doors of the museum, they implied, was going not only to undermine Narkompros's core mission, but also to present the fledgling Soviet art establishment in a poor light to the international artistic community. Apparently the threat worked, because the Museum of Painterly Culture was allowed to remain open. However, the museum never received the promised funds for its operating budget, which led Rodchenko to complain: "We have no money and [everything] is broken."[63]

Little did the museum's prospects improve by the late fall of 1921, when the Museum Bureau and the Museum of Painterly Culture found themselves subordinated to the newly created Main Scientific Administration, the self-proclaimed "scientific, ideological, and administrative organ of Narkompros." The creation of this new unit was part of yet another Narkompros reorganization that replaced the "Academic Center" with the Main Scientific Administration (see figure 2). The Main Scientific Administration was responsible for executing "leadership, control, and coordination of

Figure 2. Art Institutions Within Narkompros After 1922 Reorganization

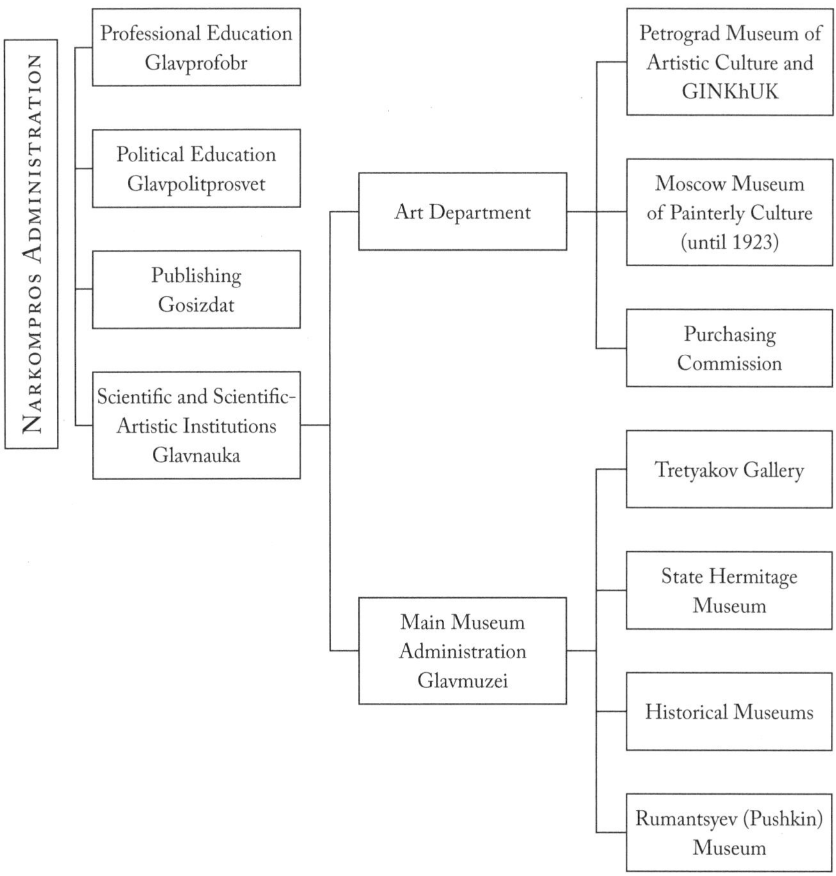

all activity" of its "academies, scientific centers, research institutions, [and] art . . . institutions" through its four main divisions: Art, Museum, Science, and a division of General oversight.[64] The Main Scientific Administration's Art Division, for example, was charged with imposing a "single plan and method"[65] on art departments, which had previously been divided into separate administrations that tended to act as autonomous units. The division coordinated all activities related to art, organized new art institutions, and controlled which institutions received state funds, as well as how those funds were deployed. Since the administrators at the Main Scientific Administration expected the institutions under their supervision to be more rigorously research-oriented, the survival of a particular art establishment depended on its director's ability to find new patrons in Narkompros and convince them of the utility of his or her unit's creative output.

The unit responsible for wielding financial and administrative control over the activities of the Moscow Museum of Painterly Culture was the Main Scientific Administration's Art Division, which was headed by Mikhail Rodionov (1907–1950). As Lunacharsky became increasingly unavailable and remote, Rodionov assumed the role of an able middleman between art institutions and the bureaucratic apparatus. His patronage over the next four years was an important factor in the survival of the Moscow Museum of Painterly Culture. Indeed, in the recounting of the museum's difficult history, Rodionov, rather than Lunacharsky, emerges as an important ally and patron of this fledgling institution. While Rodionov had the perfect reasons and opportunity to shut down the entire operation in 1922—it was temporarily closed, it had no funds, and it was ideologically suspect—in December 1922 and in January and February 1923, Rodionov demanded and received additional funds for the Museum of Painterly Culture, since the funds allotted to the museum by the Main Scientific Administration were insufficient.[66]

In December 1921, Rodchenko reported to his new boss at the Main Scientific Administration that the Museum of Painterly Culture was "all packed up" and that "objects which undoubtedly have and will have colossal value are located in crates." He continued: "I consider it impossible to bear further responsibility for the murderous policy of the slow ruination of artworks in the collection of the museum."[67] However, Rodchenko not only stopped short of resigning his directorship, but also soon submitted a carefully worded budget request that described the museum as "an institution of a scientific character, where theoretical questions about museums are worked out."[68] Significantly, this document mentioned neither contemporary art nor its educational value for the proletariat. In fact, the language of Rodchenko's request for funds for 1922 represented almost a complete renunciation of the original plan for the Moscow Museum of Painterly Culture, and a significant revision from the goals that he had helped to formulate just one year earlier. This shift in policy can be explained by two factors: first, the museum's new administrative home within the Main Scientific Administration; and second, Rodchenko's own view of the museum as a laboratory. The term "scientific" was now defined beyond technological progress or laboratory research, to signify any enterprise promoting objective, progressive work that would benefit the cultural, political, or economic realm of Soviet life. The term "scientific worker" described those carrying out research work in research establishments, as well as research and teaching work in colleges and institutes, irrespective of whether they had a postgraduate degree or academic title. Furthermore, the term applied to "specialists" (including artists) carrying out work on projects and project design. Despite this prescriptive definition, however, many "scientific workers" were actually engaged in the humanities. Even art could be considered a kind of "soft science" in the Marxist program.[69]

If anyone could convince the Main Scientific Administration that the Museum of Painterly Culture's collection of vanguard art was truly Soviet, it was Rodchenko—the modernist artist who actually managed to establish a distinctive mode of making Soviet vanguard art. Rodchenko began formulating the theory and practice of Constructivism, a rational, materialist, utilitarian approach to socially committed art,[70] at the same time as he became head of the Museum Bureau, responsible for writing reports about the Museum of Painterly Culture's activities.[71] In November 1920, Rodchenko became instructor of "construction" at VKhUTEMAS, and, later that same month, formed the "General Working Group of Objective Analysis" together with Stepanova and the sculptor Alexei Babichev (1887–1963). This was the origin of the "First Working Group of Constructivists," which came to include Rodchenko, Stepanova, Alexei Gan (1893–1942), Georgy and Vladimir Sternberg, Boris Ioganson (1893–1973), and Konstantin Medunetsky (1899–1935), all of whom not only helped to formulate the basic tenets of Constructivism, but also went on to exhibit their "spatial constructions" (see figure 3) within the Museum of Painterly Culture, in a room devoted to "experimental techniques."[72] In a clear-cut case of cross-pollination, ideas being worked out within these "Constructivist" discussion groups informed decisions that Rodchenko made as museum director, and, conversely, the science-inflected discourse that he used to explain the museum's activities for Soviet bureaucrats helped to shape the "experimental" nature of Constructivist "laboratory work." So when Rodchenko described the Moscow Museum of Painterly Culture as "an institution of scientific character, where theoretical questions about museum construction are

Figure 3. Konstantin Medunetsky, *Spatial Construction*. 1920. Tin, brass, iron, and aluminum. 45 cm. Yale University Art Gallery. Gift of Collection Société Anonyme.

worked out," he was not just paying lip service to the Main Scientific Administration. He was helping to invent the very language used to describe Bolshevik "museology." As Maria Gough contends, "Rodchenko's museological model severed the fundamental connection between history and the museum. . . . by elaborating an entirely new function for the museum—that of a historyless laboratory of living forms, wherein the subject of art was its own production."[73] Rodchenko's adoption of the discourse of technology, industry, and science, both in his verbal descriptions of the museum and in his own work, demonstrates that the modernist artist truly believed that the museum under his control could best serve as a model for the other Soviet museums if it functioned as a laboratory.

Despite the activities of its Constructivist leadership, the museum itself was foundering. Indeed Rodionov—Rodchenko's new boss as of December 1921—made his first act of patronage *not* taking any action against the Museum of Painterly Culture and its increasingly frustrated director, even though he had the perfect reason and opportunity to shut down the entire operation in 1922. A series of unpublished letters from that period attests to the dire financial situation in which the Museum of Painterly Culture found itself a year into Rodchenko's tenure, as well as to the director's valiant efforts to keep the museum open. The Moscow Museum of Painterly Culture did not function at all between late 1921 and June 1922. Its parent organization, the Museum Bureau, ceased to operate, as did the Purchasing Commission.[74] Even though the museum was not functioning, there was a full museum staff of seven people. In January 1922, Rodchenko began demanding back salaries for his employees from Rodionov. In February Rodchenko bypassed Rodionov and wrote directly to Mikhail Glibenko, the head of the Main Scientific Administration, carping about the fact that he had no telephone and that the paintings were not safe in their present accommodations. He then complained to the Main Scientific Administration that there was only cold water, no functioning toilets, and no lighting, and that the employees could not work under such conditions. He also complained about not receiving funding for museum operations, without which he could not even order stamps or paper. In fact, it was not until April 14, 1922, that the museum received 70,884,250 rubles from the Main Scientific Administration for three months' worth of back salaries.[75] In another letter addressed directly to Glibenko, Rodchenko demanded that a petition be raised in front of the Executive Committee of the Sovnarkom, the highest executive body of the Soviet state, about getting new shoes for the museum's couriers, who had to go on foot since they had no money for the tram. He even threatened to quit if Glibenko ignored his appeal.[76]

In late March 1922, having lost hope that the problems in the current space would be addressed, Rodchenko requested new accommodations for the museum. By May, he succeeded in relocating the museum, its staff, and its collections to a site on Povarskaya Street.[77] Despite the new accommodations, however, financial problems persisted. Rodchenko could not afford to install a telephone and the Main Scientific Administration refused to issue credits for it. The staff had not been paid in several months, the building was unheated, and there were no funds to buy materials necessary for displaying paintings.[78] In early May the Finance Department of the Academic Center not only denied Rodchenko's request for additional funds for salaries, but even threatened to cut back the museum's operations budget or close the museum down altogether.[79] The following week Rodchenko sent Rodionov a curt letter of protest: "I ask you to free me from the position of head of the Museum of Painterly Culture."[80] Finally, on June 19, a little less than a month before the end of the fiscal year, Rodchenko demanded that he be freed from the museum, because he was ill and going to the country for three months to recuperate.[81] Thus ended Rodchenko's brief tenure as director of the Moscow Museum of Painterly Culture. Within six months of his resignation, Rodchenko assumed the post of dean of the metalworking department at VKhUTEMAS, and symbolic of his break with the Museum of Painterly Culture, moved into a building adjacent to his new place of employment, where he would live for the rest of his life.[82]

The Moscow Museum of Painterly Culture Under Vil'yams

Discussions about Rodchenko's potential replacement were under way even before his formal break with the Museum of Painterly Culture. Shterenberg, now an arts administrator within the Main Scientific Administration, was aware of Rodchenko's series of resignations and concerned about the fate of the Moscow museum should there be no one to step into the vacated position. He notified Rodionov on June 8, 1922, that the Museum of Painterly Culture was closed because there was nobody to run it, and then nominated "young artist Comrade Vil'yams" to the post of "head of the museum."[83] Pyotr Vil'yams (1902–1947) was a politic choice to take over the museum, since he was extremely energetic, young, and not associated with prerevolutionary vanguard movements. In fact, just two years later, Vil'yams would become a cofounder of the Society of Easel Painters (Obshchestvo khudozhnikov-stankovistov, hereafter OST), a group that rejected the abstractions of Constructivism as well as nonrepresentational art, and encouraged a return to easel painting and representational art. Vil'yams's own *Portrait of V. E. Meierkhol'd* of 1925 exemplifies the aspirations of OST: a recognizable portrait of the legendary theater director, against a background of abstract geometric forms and a scaffolding-like armature that was typical of the modernist theater sets by Popova, Stepanova, and Vesnin (see figure 4). Rodionov quickly approved Shterenberg's candidate and in July 1922, at the beginning of the new fiscal year, the twenty-year-old painter became the third director of the Moscow Museum of Painterly Culture in as many years.[84] The appointment of Vil'yams, a

Figure 4. Pyotr Vil'yams, *Portrait of V. E. Meierkhol'd.* 1925. Oil on canvas. 210 × 138 cm. State Tretyakov Gallery.

friend and former student of Shterenberg at VKhUTEMAS, opened a new phase in the history of the Moscow Museum of Painterly Culture.[85] Vil'yams reoriented the Museum of Painterly Culture so it could function within the NEP environment of increased ideological control and decreased state funding.[86] Now the Moscow Museum of Painterly Culture faced a set of formidable and conflicting tasks: conform to ideological demands of the Main Scientific Administration, yet appeal to popular taste; live up to specific expectations of a "scientific-artistic" institution, yet remain unique to avoid closure due to "parallelism." This is the circle that Vil'yams had to square as soon as he took over the directorship of the Museum of Painterly Culture. Although the character of the museum was altered under his leadership, Vil'yams's ability to compromise allowed the museum to become a sovietized repository of modern art, and therefore function with a greater degree of normalcy.

In the short interval between October 1922 and May 1923, when he was abruptly demoted to deputy director, Vil'yams successfully retooled the Museum of Painterly Culture as an exhibition space with educational ambitions, as a research institution, and as a self-supporting business venture. In his October 1922 report to the Art Department of the Main Scientific Administration, Vil'yams announced that the museum had reopened on October 15, 1922, and that on Wednesdays, "those wishing to acquaint themselves with the new trends in painting" could come for an excursion. The list of artists on display included modernists of various persuasions: Shterenberg, Tatlin, Rodchenko, Udal'tsova, Larionov, Goncharova, Rozanova, Popova, Kuznetsov; Vassily Rozhdestvensky (1884–1963), a founding member of the Jack of Diamonds; Mikhail Le Dantiu (1891–1917), an active member of the prerevolutionary "Union of Youth"; and Vera Pestel' (1887–1952), an early adherent of Suprematism and then member of the "Makovets" group.[87] In the same report, Vil'yams also boasted about the fact that within one month of his appointment, the museum had successfully negotiated for more space and that the Museum of Painterly Culture's financial situation had improved to the point where there were even funds for acquisitions.[88] However, the optimistic tone of Vil'yams's first report to the Main Scientific Administration belied the fact that the museum had been on the verge of relocation to the provinces just one month earlier, and that the Museum of Painterly Culture only managed to remain in Moscow because of a series of well-directed petitions from influential members of the Art Workers' Union (Soyuz rabochikh iskusstv, henceforth known as RABIS) and VKhUTEMAS, where many of Moscow's modernists taught.[89]

In the director's report submitted to the Main Scientific Administration's Art Department in December 1922, Vil'yams described the programs and activities sponsored by members of the new Museum Council: Nina Kogan (1889–1942), a passionate adherent of Suprematism from Vitebsk; Solomon Nikritin (1898–1965), a former VKhUTEMAS student; Alexander Tyshler (1898–1980), another Ukrainian-born VKhUTEMAS student and a future member of the Society of Easel Painters; Udal'tsova, who would also soon join OST; and, of course, the cofounder of OST, Vil'yams himself.[90] As this list of council members suggests, the network of Constructivists—Rodchenko, Stepanova, Drevin—was replaced by yet another loosely knit group of young artists determined to create modernist Soviet art using the Museum of Painterly Culture as their administrative home. In their capacity as members of the Museum Council, Vil'yams and his colleagues organized a series of lectures for the public on questions of contemporary art, managed the "research" sector of the institution, and acted as the ideological steering committee of the museum. At the formal opening of the museum on December 3, they staged an art exhibition that served to emphasize the variety of schools and methods of painting represented in the museum's collection, making sure to include examples of everything from Impressionism to Suprematism.[91] In a description sent to the Main Scientific Administration soon after this event, Vil'yams underlined the Museum Council's efforts to create a Soviet context for the Museum of Painterly Culture's collection of vanguard art and explained, in what he believed was appropriately materialist language, that the purpose of his museum was "research in the area of the *science of fine art* [emphasis mine] from a purely theoretical point of view, namely, on questions of form, questions of material, its arrangement, approaches to the development of art, and also theoretical questions of composition, etc."[92]

Whether the Main Scientific Administration officials who had to read Vil'yams's statement of purpose actually understood it as an expression of scientific materialism mattered less, at this stage, than the Museum of Painterly Culture's ability to fulfill its obligation to generate enough income to cover its own operating expenses and acquisitions. This economic imperative determined the Museum of Painterly Culture's activities for the first half of 1923. In January 1923, the Museum Council staged an exhibition devoted solely to Malevich. Admission fees were charged and Vil'yams described Malevich's ouevre as demonstrating the path of the development of contemporary artists, thus fulfilling an educational function. A series of lectures was organized in connection with the exhibition, including one by Malevich himself.[93] Other revenue-generating activities specifically approved by the Main Scientific Administration included the printing and sale of *Zangezi*,[94] the Futurist play by the late Velimir Khlebnikov (1885–1922); guided tours;[95] and the deaccession of some "undesirable" objects.[96] In addition to the lecture series and guided tours, Vil'yams's March 1923 report of museum activities also mentioned two successful exhibitions, as well as exchanges with other museums. In short, by seeking the middle ground and by placing his collection of vanguard art in an appropriately "scientific" and educational context, Vil'yams had initiated what was without doubt the liveliest period of museum activity in the Museum of Painterly Culture's brief and rather spotty history.

The Moscow Museum of Painterly Culture Under Vainer

In May 1923, in an effort to "unite the . . . activity of all scientific-artistic institutions of the RSFSR,"[97] the Museum of Painterly Culture was abruptly transferred from the Art Department of the Main Scientific Administration to the Main Museum Administration (Glavnoe muzeinoe upravlenie, hereafter Glavmuzei); and Lazar Vainer (1885–1933), a realist sculptor, Communist Party member since 1917, and former Main Scientific Administration inspector, was named director of the Museum of Painterly Culture.[98] Since its founding as the Department of Preservation,[99] the Main Museum Administration had been, perhaps unsurprisingly, artistically conservative. Its employees included Abram Efros and Igor Grabar, two former members of the 1919 joint departmental "contact committee," who were also known for their skepticism of the kind of modernist experimentation that was characteristic of the "lefts" in art. Although the Main Museum Administration was officially under the Main Scientific Administration, this unit enjoyed the support of the Sovnarkom, which held as a tenet central to Marxism-Leninism the belief that "museums are powerful centers of worker and peasant education, and are also important for the education of national minorities."[100] The Main Museum Administration's political connections and status as a centerpiece of Marxist-Leninist ideology translated into economic security: this division of the Main Scientific Administration was consistently allotted twice the credits and funds of other Soviet arts organizations.

While the reasons for the transfer of the Museum of Painterly Culture were never elucidated, it appears that this bureaucratic reshuffle had less to do with Vil'yams's abilities, or the Moscow museum's ideological stance, than with interdepartmental rivalry, specifically the Main Museum Administration officials' desire to take over the management of the Moscow Museum of Painterly Culture from their colleagues in the Art Division, ostensibly to bring this art institution's activities in line with the Main Museum Administration's own policies regarding the museums of Soviet Russia. Spurred by this bureaucratic defeat, Mikhail Rodionov, the head of the Main Scientific Administration's Art Department, wrote two impassioned letters protesting the Museum of Painterly Culture's transfer and Vil'yams's replacement. In the first letter, dated May 15 and addressed to the "head of the Main Scientific Administration" (Mikhail Glibenko), Rodionov expressed dismay at this decision, especially since it was made and executed entirely without his involvement, while he was away in Petrograd. Rodionov argued that the real value of the Moscow Museum of Painterly Culture lay in its uniqueness as an art institution, that is, "an institution that not only preserves works of art, like an ordinary museum, but that illustrates constant movement and development of artistic culture in its current achievements." He also objected to the egregious mismatch of the museum with Vainer, a "sculptor of the realist trend, the so-called 'right school,'" who, Rodionov maintained, "does not have any ideological connection with the contents of the Museum (Left painting) and with the direction of all former activities of the museum." He expressed regret that this move "undoubtedly will entail the inevitable alteration of the work of the museum" and concluded that the appointment of Vainer was a "mistake," especially in view of that fact that "Comrade Vil'yams" was a "wonderful worker" who was undeservedly demoted.[101]

Rodionov's second letter, which was addressed to Lunacharsky, the head of Narkompros, echoed these sentiments, but defended the Museum of Painterly Culture's unique contribution to the Soviet art world even more vociferously than the first:

> Most esteemed Anatoly Vasilievich.
>
> The two Museums of Artistic Culture [in Moscow and Petrograd] were created by David Petrovich Shterenberg . . . and have distinguished themselves from the usual type of museum, [which is] a storehouse. Until recently, the museums were under the Main Scientific Administration's Art Department and I personally expended not a little energy to save the Moscow museum from collapse and then to help organize it in a new location. For the last year . . . under comrade Vil'yams . . . a young artist, who not long ago graduated from VKhUTEMAS, the situation of the museum and its activity has improved extraordinarily. The new director [Vainer] has absolutely no ideas in common with the original ideas on the basis of which the museum was created . . . I consider it my duty to bring this matter to your attention. The Museum of Painterly Culture . . . will not preserve its previous character and will not be guaranteed its independence. The situation is especially dangerous because the new head has nothing in common with the Museum . . . He may be very talented, but in other areas. [Since] the Museum of Artistic Culture was a citadel of the so-called Left front . . . the nomination can hardly be called successful. The transfer of the Museum to the management of the Museum Administration may be expedient, but in my opinion only under the condition of some kind of guarantee that the Museum preserves the ideology of its founders.[102]

This previously unpublished piece of internal correspondence between the head of the Main Scientific Administration's Art Department and the people's commissar of enlightenment offers a perfect illustration of the curious way in which bureaucratic politics and artistic ideals were intertwined during the period of the New Economic Policy. For although the correspondence between Rodionov and Lunacharsky does attest to the gradual homogenization and centralization of cultural life, it would not be quite accurate to describe the Museum of Painterly Culture's outmaneuvered patron as a defender of artistic pluralism, or his rivals at the Main Museum Administration as the forces of uniformity. Rodionov's eventual fate does, however, suggest that the head of the Main Scientific Administration's Art Department did pay a price for his outspoken defense of an ideologically suspect institution: in early 1924, after barely a year as departmental director, he was demoted to assistant head.

As Rodionov had predicted, the transfer to the Main Museum Administration represented a serious blow both to the Museum of Painterly Culture's autonomy and to its uniqueness as a champion of vanguard art in a Soviet context. However, this move also presented new opportunities. Lazar Vainer turned out to be a good administrator with excellent connections, which he used not only to advance the museum's critical educational role within the larger network of Soviet museums, but also to encourage new trends in Soviet modernism. At the end of May, after one month as director of the Museum of Painterly Culture, Vainer appealed to the director of the Main Museum Administration for larger accommodations for exhibitions, lectures, permanent laboratories, and a library.[103] His request was granted and, during the summer, the Museum of Painterly Culture was relocated for a second time since its founding. However, at the end of 1923, the museum was forced out of its new accommodations by the Higher Literary Institute, and it had to be relocated yet again, this time to the VKhUTEMAS building at 11 Rozhdestvenka.[104] In a feeble attempt to remain faithful to the founders' goal of focusing on the technical aspects of vanguard painting, rather than on its content, the collection of three hundred works of modern art was divided into two formal categories—"volumetric" and "flat"—and distributed among the six rooms that constituted the entire exposition space at VKhUTEMAS. Despite such cramped quarters, the museum, which reopened by July 1924, could once again serve a dual purpose: as an exhibition space devoted to "a complete collection of contemporary Russian masters from Mashkov to Malevich,"[105] as well as a laboratory for the creation of a particularly Soviet brand of modernist art.

In addition to reinstalling the collection at its new location on Rozhdestvenka, the Museum of Painterly Culture continued to send paintings to regional museums: in November 1923, for example, the Main Museum Administration told Vainer to select and send some works from the collection to an unspecified provincial museum, and another group of works to the Tretyakov Gallery.[106] The Museum of Painterly Culture staff also engaged in a wide range of other activities, from organizing a library to opening a research lab, where "scientific employees" worked on "painting methods" and "demonstrated new artistic methods."[107] This undoubtedly referred to the work being carried out in the museum's studios, or "laboratories," by the future members of OST, who continued to control the Museum Council and who succeeded in turning the Moscow Museum of Painterly Culture into their art organization's informal home by 1925.[108] The Museum of Painterly Culture exhibited the work of OST and its precursor the Projectionists on four occasions between 1925 and 1928. Vil'yams's *Portrait of V. E. Meierkhol'd* of 1925 represents the typical visual language adopted by these artists, all of whom employed a representational yet modernist pictorial idiom. By depicting socialist content (factories, workers, cities, soldiers) in a modernist visual idiom, members of the Museum Council, such as Vil'yams, Tyshler, Nikritin, and Alexander Labas (1900–1983), attempted to create an appropriate type of painting for the new society, one that was distinct from the abstractions of Constructivism and the didactic realism of the Association of Artists of Revolutionary Russia (Assosiatsiya khudozhnikov revoliutsionnoi rossii, hereafter AKhRR).[109] As Charlotte Douglas has pointed out, the emergence of a particularly Soviet modernist language was indeed fostered by OST's association with the Museum of Painterly Culture.[110]

Success as innovative Soviet artists, however, did not shield the Museum of Painterly Culture staff from additional, unplanned, administrative reorganizations. When Deputy Director Vil'yams submitted a budget request for the 1924–25 academic year, for example, he had no idea that for the first six months of 1924 the museum would remain essentially closed.[111] It is also unclear whether he or anyone else on the Museum of Painterly Culture Museum Board was ever consulted before the Main Museum Administration announced, in October 1924, that the Moscow Museum of Painterly Culture had become a branch of the State Tretyakov Gallery.[112] Officials at the Main Museum Administration envisioned the Tretyakov Gallery—the largest and most comprehensive collection of Russian art in Moscow, which was nationalized by the Soviet government "because of its cultural and artistic significance . . . in the interests of the working classes" and placed under the People's Commissariat of Enlightenment in June 1918—as the central museum of Russian art, with other art museums as branches.[113] Vainer remained the director of the Museum of Painterly Culture, and Vil'yams deputy director, but their institution was now financially and ideologically accountable to the directorship of the Tretyakov, which had its own budget and was only nominally administered by the Main Museum Administration, an institution that in just three years would itself be rendered obsolete by the creation of an overarching Main Arts Administration (Glavnoe upravlenie iskusstva, hereafter Glaviskusstvo).

At this juncture both Vil'yams and Vainer realized that the museum's survival depended on presenting itself as having a unique educational function within the Soviet cultural arena. Immediately after the announcement, Vainer, Vil'yams, and two modernists, Aristarkh Lentulov (1882–1943) and Robert Fal'k (1886–1958), met to discuss efforts to enhance the Museum of Painterly Culture's role as a cultural-educational institution, one that was not only aligned with the goals of Soviet art administrators, but also committed to engaging Soviet audiences. Among other things, they discussed two of Vainer's suggestions: first, that every work of art displayed in the museum should be accompanied by explanatory material and the general goals of the artist, since "every master should and can work not only with a brush but with a pen"; and second, that all groups should say something definite about their artistic methods to create a unified "ideological front" for the museum. This, Vainer believed, would end the general "muddle" in contemporary art.[114] Although it is not clear whether Vainer's ideas were ever actually implemented, the general pedagogical orientation adopted after the Museum of Painterly Culture's incorporation into the administrative structure of the Tretyakov Gallery actually did save the museum from closing its doors. In fact, the Museum of Painterly Culture was able to stave off eviction from the VKhUTEMAS building in December 1924 precisely because Vil'yams could convince the Main Scientific Administration's Scholarly Council of the museum's cultural-educational importance to the students at VKhUTEMAS, 1,700 of whom had, by the deputy director's count, visited the museum in 1924.[115]

Although the Museum of Painterly Culture remained open, in March 1925 its entire collection was transferred to the premises of the State Tretyakov Gallery.[116] This move further eroded the museum's autonomy, but the transfer also lifted the burden of storage and preservation of about three hundred works from the shoulders of the museum staff.[117] This relocation also meant that the more ample space could be used to exhibit the works of art being created by members of the Museum Council, such as Nikritin, Tyshler, Labas, and Vil'yams. Indeed, the years 1925–26 turned out to be the board members' most active period, with an ambitious exhibition schedule and lively pedagogical programming. Vil'yams's report to the Tretyakov Gallery administration for that fiscal year dutifully opened with a description of the "scientific" nature of the museum's work—the classification of types of painting, the creation of tables denoting elements of form and color, and the elaboration of "methods of quantitative analysis" of form—which was being carried out in the Analytical Department and the Experimental Department.[118] However, most of the report actually focused on successful examples of instruction and outreach, such as "analyzing compositions [from the time] of old master [painting] until works of today" and "organizing traveling exhibitions around Moscow worker clubs and giving accompanying explanatory lectures," that is, educational activities that sought to contextualize and, as much as possible, popularize the modernist art in the Museum of Painterly Culture's collection.[119] Similarly, in an effort to increase use of the over five hundred monographs and journals that had been collected by the Department of Fine Arts, Vil'yams successfully petitioned the Tretyakov administration for help in maintaining and even expanding the Museum of Painterly Culture's specialized art library, arguing that "collecting the latest Russian and foreign publications on art" enhanced the museum's function as an educational center.[120] During these busy years, Vil'yams boasted that 3,733 people visited the museum and that the Museum of Painterly Culture staff led over twenty guided tours of its galleries.[121] Assuming that these numbers are fairly accurate, the Museum of Painterly Culture was taking in more money from the paying public than from the state, a fact which may explain why the Museum Council could use its own funds to pay the artists employed in the museum.[122]

Even more impressive than the frequency of public lectures organized by the Museum of Painterly Culture or the size of its library holdings was the number of art exhibitions mounted in 1925 and 1926. Gallery shows included a "purely retrospective" exhibit called "Left Trends of the Last Fifteen Years"; an exhibit devoted to the realist group "Makovets"; and a showing of the works of the "Moscow Society of Painters," which was composed of such diverse artists as former Jack of Diamonds artists Fal'k, Konchalovsky, Grabar, and Udal'tsova.[123] Considering the composition of the Museum of Painterly Culture's own Museum Council, it is not surprising that two whole exhibits were devoted to the work produced by members of OST. And although Lazar Vainer had been initially cast by Rodionov as having "nothing in common" with the Museum of Painterly Culture, he did become a member of the Museum of Painterly Culture network, exhibiting his sculptures in two OST exhibits in 1925 and 1926, and even creating a sculpture of his comrade Pyotr Vil'yams.[124] What is surprising is the enormous amount of time that these artists devoted to producing easel paintings for increasingly more frequent exhibitions and sales. Unlike their counterparts in Leningrad, the modernists employed by the Moscow Museum of Painterly Culture appeared to be less intent on creating works as part of their own "research" projects than on being on view at such events as the 1924 "First Discussional Exhibition," which included the work of Museum of Painterly Culture Council members Nikritin, Tyshler, Udal'tsova, and Vil'yams; the 1924 Venice Biennale, which included works by Shterenberg and Vil'yams; and the 1926 exhibition in Tokyo, in which all working artists in Moscow were represented.[125] The fact that many of the works completed by the Museum of Painterly Culture's own employees were exhibited and even sold to the recently revived Purchasing Commission suggests that at this moment in its history, despite Vil'yams's assertions to the contrary, the survival of the Moscow museum did not actually depend on its scientific or scholarly character. Indeed, the description of research projects being carried out in museum laboratories found in Vil'yams's annual report was apparently specious, since no real laboratories could be found on the museum's premises.[126] His use of science-inflected rhetoric can thus best be described as a pragmatic move meant to protect the particular network of artists employed in the museum and to allow them to develop their own brand of Soviet modernism, all under the watchful eye of the Tretyakov Gallery administration.

The Museum of Painterly Culture's rationale in what turned out to be its final incarnation thus appears to have been the promotion and exhibition of a particular brand of Soviet modernism. Under the leadership of Vainer and Vil'yams, the Museum Council pursued a policy that sought to position the Museum of Painterly Culture as a unique, and uniquely Soviet, cultural heritage institution, one that filled an important niche due to its preoccupation with cultural enlightenment and issues relating solely to contemporary art, especially art produced by graduates from VKhUTEMAS, for whom "contemporary art" no longer meant "Futurist" or nonobjective art, but rather new versions of realist easel painting. The Museum of Painterly Culture staked everything on its connection to VKhUTEMAS students, who frequented the library and exhibition space to see the work of their teachers and contemporaries, and that gamble may have paid off handsomely in the future. But fate, and the heavy-handedness of the Tretyakov administration, intervened to forestall this option. Had it not been for a hair salon that operated in the vestibule of the Moscow Museum of Painterly Culture during off-hours, or to the salon patrons' insistence on using the museum's bathrooms thereby jeopardizing the safety of the works of art, the Museum of Painterly Culture may have been able to remain in its location proximate to VKhUTEMAS.[127] But rather than shutting down the salon and restricting museum access only to its own employees, the Tretyakov administration opted instead to relocate the Museum of Painterly Culture to the site of the former Stroganov School, a space earlier occupied by the Museum of

Asian Arts.[128] Vainer vociferously protested his supervisors' decision on the grounds that his museum and its library were "closely connected with the work of VKhUTEMAS" and, therefore, should logically be in the same building as the art school. But for the first time since his appointment to the directorship, Vainer's contacts in the Main Museum Administration failed to come through: his protests went unnoticed, and the Museum of Painterly Culture was forced to move in September 1926.[129] This move, and the others that soon followed, undermined the unique institutional identity that the Museum of Painterly Culture had worked so hard to create and advertise in its annual reports to Soviet art administrators and severed the connections that it so carefully cultivated with VKhUTEMAS.[130] As a result, the Museum of Painterly Culture appeared to lose both its identity and its raison d'être.

There is little documentary material relating to the activities of the Museum of Painterly Culture between fall 1926 and the time of its eventual closing in early 1929. The extant archival record, however, does reveal an intense debate regarding the museum's location, its intended function, and even its right to exist. The museum was relocated at least two more times between October 1926 and October 1928, causing inevitable disruptions of its activities.[131] Despite these disruptions, the museum staff—now consisting solely of Vainer, Vil'yams, and Nikritin—somehow managed to mount three more OST exhibitions. In 1927, the Museum of Painterly Culture also participated in a large exhibition organized by the Tretyakov Gallery in honor of the tenth anniversary of the October Revolution. The Museum of Painterly Culture was specifically charged with "explanation of the collection, lectures, and speeches," all of which were to be carried out under the supervision of Narkompros employees.[132] In August 1928, the Museum of Painterly Culture even appeared to have found a new champion in Mikhail Kristi (1875–1956), a top administrator at the recently formed Main Arts Administration, who would soon go on to serve two terms as director of the State Tretyakov Gallery (1928–32 and 1934–37).[133] Kristi not only affirmed the Museum of Painterly Culture's right to operate under the aegis of the Tretyakov Gallery, but also noted that the museum "has great significance as a research institution."[134]

Just two months later, however, the question of "the future work of the Museum of Painterly Culture" once again became the subject of discussion, this time at a meeting of the Main Arts Administration's Department of Fine Arts. This departmental meeting was attended by Alexei Fedorov-Davydov (1900–1969), art historian, museologist, and longtime nemesis of "futurist" art; Ivan Matsa [János Mácza] (1893–1974), a Hungarian-born Marxist critic; Alfred Kurella (1895–1975), a German-born Soviet citizen, who was active in the Soviet art and literature apparatus; Ignaty Khvoinik, who published works of art criticism between 1921 and 1935; and two of the three remaining members of the Museum of Painterly Culture's Council, Pyotr Vil'yams and Solomon Nikritin. Noticeably absent from this meeting was the last "head curator" of the Museum of Painterly Culture, who by then had managed to obtain a position as assistant head of the Main Scientific Administration's Museum Department.[135] While none of the attendees at the October 1928 meeting called for the museum's closing, they all agreed that substantial changes had to take place, starting with the creation of research laboratories, which "until now, are not found" in the museum. However, they made no recommendations other than that the Museum of Painterly Culture should be considered an "experimental museum, which should carry out definite experimental work," yet remain entirely accountable to the Main Arts Administration and the administration of the Tretyakov Gallery. Fedorov-Davydov was charged with creating a new charter for the museum, but no director was named. Before they adjourned the meeting, the members of the Department of Fine Arts agreed to "raise the question about the Museum of Painterly Culture in the near future."[136] However, they appear never to have followed up on this resolution, and the paper trail for the Museum of Painterly Culture comes to an abrupt halt after December 1928, the date when the museum can be said to have effectively ceased to operate as a separate unit within the organizational structure of the Tretyakov Gallery.[137]

One of the last official documents related to the Moscow Museum of Painterly Culture, an internal report written by an unidentified Main Arts Administration employee sometime before the end of 1928, reveals the extent to which this modernist outpost had been "sovietized" during the period of the New Economic Policy. In this document, and for the first time in its history, the Museum of Painterly Culture was referred to as the "State Museum of Artistic Culture"—a designation that brought this institution's nomenclature in line with the one to which it reported, the "State" Tretyakov Gallery. More substantively, the Main Arts Administration's report went on to describe the Museum of Painterly Culture as an "experimental laboratory" concerned with new types of museum expositions.[138] This description was not altogether different from the vision articulated by some of the Museum of Painterly Culture's original founders, who, as we have seen, saw the Moscow museum as the locus for the creation of a new type of museological practice, wherein artists themselves were responsible for the management of the museum, and one that was appropriately research-oriented for the Soviet era. And it certainly fitted nicely into the historical trajectory traced in Vil'yams's final report as assistant to the chief curator of the Museum of Painterly Culture, which was also written in 1928.

Vil'yams's historical narrative was organized into three "stages," a schema that perhaps not coincidentally echoed Karl Marx's famous formulation of the three stages of Communism. During the first, "revolutionary" stage of the museum's history (1919–21), Vil'yams argued, the Museum of Painterly Culture was "only a collection of contemporary Russian painting," an institution whose sole task was the organization of exhibitions. During the second stage (1921–25), corresponding to Marx's "transitional phase," the Museum of Painterly Culture began to do "concrete forms of laboratory work" and to fulfill an educational mission. The third stage (1925–28), corresponding to Marx's Communist "utopia," was, according to Vil'yams, the period in which taxonomic and investigative research and cultural education were the defining missions of the museum; or, as he himself put it, the Museum of Painterly Culture had "evolved into a scientific-research and scientific-educational institution with the goal of establishing a scientific-pedagogical method of art study," a turn of phrase that reveals the former deputy director's skill at adopting the language of officialdom—a skill that he developed not only while creating his Soviet modernist paintings, but also while functioning as a bureaucrat, writing the correspondence and annual reports that kept the Museum of Painterly Culture open and its experimental "laboratories" working.[139] Viewed from this perspective, the Museum of Painterly Culture had reached its final stage of development: by 1928, it had become—at least on paper—a model Soviet institution. While the functions of the museum in its last iteration were different—originally the Museum of Painterly Culture was devoted solely to display, while the "State Museum of Artistic Culture" was supposed to be devoted to the development of materialist museum methods and theory—the organization as a whole had come to embody the very notions of dialectical development and progress for which the Bolshevik Revolution was made, and therefore, Vil'yams implied, could not simply be dissolved. Obviously, his superiors in the Main Arts Administration thought otherwise and the Museum of Painterly Culture was simply allowed to wither away. But, as the aforementioned 1928 Main Arts Administration report suggests, not before the last group of artists within the museum had begun to put into practice some of the very same ideas that had been promulgated by modernist artists in 1918 and 1919.

The fate of the Museum of Painterly Culture during what Vil'yams called its third, "utopian" stage, confirms recent assessments of early Soviet culture, especially during the period known as the New Economic Policy.[140] As other scholars have argued, this period of supposedly utopian experimentation and pluralism actually witnessed the development of two important national trends: first, standardization and homogenization of the intelligentsia and the institutions in which they worked; and second, the increased role of a formidable, centralized administrative apparatus that governed all artistic enterprises well before Stalin's infamous 1932 decree banning all independent art groups and activities. However, as I have tried to emphasize, if we focus only on the last three years of this story, we will wind up downplaying the resourcefulness of Russia's modernist artists, who not only managed to create works of enduring interest and value under incredibly difficult material conditions and in an increasingly hostile ideological and political environment; but also, by their own actions as arts administrators, helped to formulate and apply the very language and practices that came to characterize the bureaucratic apparatus of the early Soviet state. Indeed, the fact that the Museum of Painterly Culture survived the first ten years of Soviet rule is a testament to its four directors' abilities to create and re-create an appropriate context for modernist experimentation that relied upon and, in turn, helped to shape Bolshevik rhetoric and ideology as it evolved in the early Soviet period. Not only were these directors making modernist art Soviet, but in the case of Rodchenko, Vainer, and Vil'yams, they were actually facilitating the creation of a particularly Soviet modernism.

Chapter Two

The Center of Artistic Life: The People's School of Art in Vitebsk, 1919–1923

It is well known that for a brief but incandescent moment in the history of Russian modernism, the People's School of Art (Narodnoe khudozhestvennoe uchilishche) in Vitebsk,[1] a provincial city on the far western boundary of the Russian Soviet Federative Socialist Republic (RSFSR),[2] became the institutional home to such luminaries as Marc Chagall, El Lissitzky, and Kazimir Malevich. What is less well known, and what this chapter will examine, is how the artists who worked and taught in this haven of modernist experimentation dealt with the deluge of decrees issuing from the Soviet capital, as well as the extent to which their efforts allowed this progressive art school to survive at a time when nearly half of all the region's cultural institutions were shut down. The role played by Malevich and the "Supporters of the New Art" (Utverditeli novogo iskusstva, hereafter UNOVIS), particularly during the two-year period when Vera Ermolaeva (1893–1938) served as the art school's rector, was crucial to this short-lived success story.[3] As we will see, under the spiritual guidance of the founder of Suprematism,[4] Ermolaeva adapted the school's program so that it would become a model Soviet art school, one that stressed materialist approaches to the study of art and concretely contributed to the construction of socialism while simultaneously retaining its commitment to training students in techniques of modern—even nonrepresentational—art. By integrating the principles of UNOVIS, and its members' commitment to abstraction into the school curriculum, the administration of the People's School of Art succeeded in presenting their students and faculty as activist artists within a socialist society, and their artistic program as a socially transformative, radical critique of capitalist modes of artistic production, in which a collective of artists carried out projects that participated in and met the needs of the socialist state. In doing so, the Vitebsk modernists not only skillfully promoted socialist methods and values like their capital-dwelling counterparts, but also contributed to the "sovietization" of Suprematism itself.

Marc Chagall and the Origins of the People's School of Art

The fact that Vitebsk, a small, provincial city in the former Pale of Settlement, should become a vibrant artistic center was due as much to the presence of Yehuda Pen's School of Painting and Drawing as to the purposeful decentralization of cultural life that occurred at Narkompros's behest during the early Soviet era, in an attempt to redress "cultural deprivation" in the provinces.[5] A professionally trained artist with the rank of academician, Yehudah Pen (1854–1937) taught hundreds of art students, including Osip Zadkine (1890–1967), El Lissitzky (1890–1941), and most notably Marc Chagall (1887–1985). At the time of the Russian Revolution, Pen had about thirty students in his school, which he operated out of his apartment.[6] In September 1918, Anatoly Lunacharsky, the commissar of enlightenment, persuaded Chagall—his longtime acquaintance from Paris and Petrograd—to return to his place of birth and become the commissar of arts for the Vitebsk region.[7] Chagall's duties were to include administration of all artistic life in the region, including the fine arts, music, and theater.[8] Regardless of whether the newly christened arts commissar was "filled with enthusiasm"[9] at the prospect of "introducing the poor children of the city to art,"[10] as some sources would have it, Chagall's brief stint of employment in the Soviet state bureaucracy was typical of the wider migration of vanguard artists to government positions, a move that, as we saw in the previous chapter, was driven as much by pragmatism as idealism.

Chagall's second task after his return to Vitebsk—the first was the decoration of the city for the anniversary of the October Revolution—was to begin the process of establishing an art school. In December 1918, Chagall published a letter in *Art of the Commune,* the short-lived newspaper edited by the Petrograd modernists, exhorting art teachers to "leave the Capital and go to the Provinces!"[11] He quickly followed up this call ("Come to us!") with the rhetorical question: "But how shall we entice you?"[12] As it turned out, Chagall need not have concerned himself about "enticing" artists to Vitebsk. The influx of artists from the two capitals had as much to do with the internal migrations caused by the Russian Civil War as with the Vitebsk arts commissar's ability to marshal the resources under his control to support like-minded colleagues and acquaintances. Between 1918 and 1920, the lack of food, fuel, consumer products, and services prompted about 700,000 urban dwellers to leave the cities for the relative security of the provinces.[13] Unlike most cities in the RSFSR, Vitebsk was a comparatively pleasant place to work and live during the first winter of the Russian Civil War. Three hundred miles southwest of Moscow, the city had food and supplies that were scarce in the capitals. Sophia Dymshits-Tolstaya, for one, would later reminisce about taking a trip to Vitebsk from Moscow for the sole purpose of obtaining food staples.[14]

The first director of the new art school was Mstislav Dobuzhinsky (1875–1957), a graphic artist best known as a founding member of the "World of Art" group. At first glance, the middle-aged Lithuanian aristocrat appeared an odd choice to direct the People's School of Art. His candidacy, however, was promoted by IZO, most likely because he had earned his revolutionary credentials with his searing antimonarchist satirical prints during the Revolution of 1905 and his energetic embrace of state commissions after the Revolution of 1917. It probably didn't hurt that between the revolutions he was also one of Chagall's favorite art teachers, having taught drawing at the school of E. N. Zvantseva in Petrograd.[15] Whether or not he had a hand in picking the head of the new art school, Chagall became intimately involved in the life of the People's School of Art. He not only served as commissar of arts for the Vitebsk region, but also taught in the painting studios alongside his other teacher, Yehudah Pen.

Other artists who answered Chagall's call at this time included the modernist painter and Malevich's friend Ivan Puni (1892–1956), and his wife, the painter and decorative arts expert Ksenia Boguslavskaya (1892–1972).[16] Vera Ermolaeva, Dobuzhinsky's eventual replacement as director of the People's School of Art, arrived in April 1919, at which point she was named the head of a painting studio and the assistant director of the school.[17] She was soon followed by Nina Kogan (1889–1942), her friend and colleague from Petrograd.[18] Both were preceded by Nadezhda Liubavina (active circa 1915–early 1920s), the youngest of this artistic triumvirate, who arrived in Vitebsk with other members of Petrograd's "artistic invasion force" on New Year's Eve 1919.[19] In May 1919, El Lissitzky relocated from Moscow, having been invited by Chagall to direct the architecture studio.[20] In turn, in October of that same year, Lissitzky invited Malevich to come and teach in the People's School of Art. Malevich accepted the offer and drafted a letter of resignation, in which he detailed his very prosaic reasons for leaving the Free Art Studios in Moscow, namely, the lack of an apartment, electricity, or even firewood to heat his cold summer cottage. He concluded, rather ruefully: "I am forced to accept the offer of the Vitebsk studios, guaranteeing me all conditions for living and working, and to give up work in Moscow."[21]

As Chagall very well knew, a vibrant artistic center needed more than a few imported teachers; it needed a museum to showcase the latest artistic developments. Indeed, the idea for a contemporary art museum in Vitebsk was broached in early February 1919, although no works were forthcoming until August 1919, when the Museum Bureau at Moscow's Museum of Painterly Culture sent paintings by Konchalovsky, Lentulov, Rodchenko, Fal'k, Le-Dantiu, Malevich, Rozanova, and other modernist artists. The Moscow-based modernists who oversaw the art purchases for the still nonexistent provincial museum also made sure to acquire works by local artists, apparently irrespective of their affiliation with any particular artistic movement. The beneficiaries of this targeted redistribution of state funds included Chagall's teacher, the academic realist Pen; Solomon Yudovin (1892–1954), a figurative artist interested in the cultural past of the Russian Jews and only minimally influenced by the latest trends; the artist and critic Alexander Romm (1887–1952), one of Chagall's oldest friends;[22] the sculptor Abram Brazer (1892–1942), an acquaintance from Chagall's stint in Paris; and of course, Chagall himself.

Despite the presence of all these works and the obvious support of the commissar of arts, however, the Vitebsk museum of contemporary art did not open to the public until July 1920. And even when it did, it had no facilities of its own. Since no other accommodations were available, the new museum had to share its display space with that of the students and teachers of the People's School of Art, which had opened more than a year earlier, on January 28, 1919, on the premises of the very same building at 10 Bukharin Street.[23]

UNOVIS: Art Party of a New Type

As Malevich's letter of resignation suggests, artists who were struggling for survival in Moscow and Petrograd welcomed, with various degrees of enthusiasm, the opportunity of joining, albeit temporarily, a network of like-minded colleagues in a more comfortable setting like Vitebsk. Malevich himself, for example, imagined only a brief sojourn in the provinces, before a planned move to Petrograd in 1920, where he already had a network of friends and supporters in place.[24] Despite his reservations, however, Malevich was characteristically active upon his arrival in Vitebsk. Although the school year was already in progress and he did not have any of his own students, Malevich used his first months in Vitebsk to publicize Suprematism and his pedagogical system, which he had started to develop in Moscow, but which, as we shall have occasion to observe later in this chapter, would receive a fresh impulse during his stint at the People's School of

Art. Within several weeks of his arrival, Malevich published a brochure on which he had been working while in Moscow, called *On New Systems of Art*, which served as a brief introduction to his philosophy.[25] Additionally, he read lectures in conjunction with an exhibition of local and Moscow artists and also participated in well-attended debates.[26] His leadership skills and personal charisma were immediately apparent to students and other faculty members, and soon had won over the majority of People's School of Art students to study the methodology and application of Suprematism.[27] By the beginning of 1920, a mere two months after Malevich's arrival in Vitebsk, a group of converts to Suprematism from among the students and teachers of the People's School of Art had established a group called the "Young Followers of New Art" (MOLPOSNOVIS), later called simply "Followers of New Art" (POSNOVIS).[28] These two organizations would in turn serve as institutional precursors to the "Supporters of the New Art" (UNOVIS), whose program was solidified by April 1920 and whose manifesto ended with the slogan "Long live the party of UNOVIS, affirming new forms of the utilitarianism of Suprematism."[29]

The triumph of Suprematism at the Vitebsk People's School of Art was formalized in July 1920, immediately after Chagall's departure from Vitebsk, when Ermolaeva, one of Malevich's most ardent followers, replaced Chagall as director of the school.[30] As a result of this quiet "coup,"[31] Malevich came to be generally acknowledged, not unjustifiably, as the "school's leading official," even though he never formally served as director of the People's School of Art.[32] During Ermolaeva's tenure, from 1920 to 1922, Malevich and the small but dedicated cohort of modern artists affiliated with UNOVIS received carte blanche to carry out their ambitious professional and pedagogical agenda. As the following extended analysis of UNOVIS members' activities, commissions, and publications will demonstrate, this agenda reveals the extent to which the self-described "party" engaged with Soviet rhetoric, ideals, and ideology. Up to now, this engagement, when it has been acknowledged at all, has generally been dismissed as mere lip service to the powers that be, or else as a simplistic reflection of the utopian spirit of the times. And utopian it surely was. Indeed, it is arguable that Suprematism, the basis for UNOVIS's creative activity, served as both a counterpoint to the chaos of the Civil War and as a bastion of hope for the future during the almost complete breakdown of society.[33] Even more boldly, the group's leaders (particularly Malevich and Lissitzky), saw Communism as merely a stop along the way to Suprematism, in much the same way that orthodox Marxists interpreted socialism as the penultimate step before the advent of Communism. Indeed, if we take Malevich at his word that "just as socialism developed in the study . . . so should our studios become the crucible in which the form of the new world will be forged,"[34] then it certainly appears that the founder of Suprematism was convinced that his system would develop alongside, but ultimately supersede, Communism as the ultimate expression of the new world.[35]

Malevich's savvy and pragmatic approach to art *and* politics after the revolution is at odds with the image of Malevich as a dreamy utopian. As Larissa Zhadova has demonstrated, however, "Malevich felt on par with inventors and scientists in engineering who produce instruments and machines"[36] and "sought the integration of art with technology and with scientific methods, and the establishment of close contacts between painters and astronomers, engineers and mechanics."[37] I would go further and argue that in his dual capacity as "party boss" and pedagogue, Malevich not only embraced the technocratic aspect of Bolshevik discourse about the construction of socialism but also consciously sought to correlate the People's School of Art's programs and curriculum with the imperatives of the early Soviet state and the ideology of the Communist Party. Indeed, the most striking feature of the vanguard "party" was how systematic and well organized it actually was. From the questionnaire that all members had to fill out, to its pedagogical goals and its energetic fulfillment of government commissions, the "Supporters of the New Art" had so many points of intersection with the Leninist "party of the new type" that it is not too much of an exaggeration to say that UNOVIS was the organizational means by which the curriculum of the People's School of Art, and Suprematism itself, became Soviet.[38]

A case in point is the questionnaire (*anketa*) that all members of UNOVIS had to fill out in the summer and fall of 1920.[39] This questionnaire not only asked members to report on their readiness to embrace the principles of UNOVIS, but also informed them of exactly what those principles were, namely, that "art schools are apparatuses for building up the culture of a new harmony of the utilitarian world of objects" and "that *partiinost'* [party-spirit or partisanship] of the school is a necessity." The questionnaire is interesting not only for its pithy expression of the UNOVIS program, but also for the fact that at exactly the same time, the Communist Party was circulating its own, new standardized questionnaire, which all members (including Lenin himself) had to fill out for reregistration in the party. Thirty-three pages in length, the Communist Party questionnaire was formulated to redress the fact that since the revolution, each region of Soviet Russia had its own application forms and party card.[40] The standardized form was intended to rectify this problem both organizationally and ideologically. To receive a new, universally valid party card (*edinnyi partiinyi bilet*), members had to fill out an official document that required them to attest to their level of commitment to the Communist Party, as well as their knowledge of its basic texts and concepts. While the UNOVIS questionnaire does not replicate the one circulated by the Bolsheviks, the intention is clearly the same: to create a dedicated core of members who shared common experiences and a common vision. In both cases, the application documents are about *partiinost'*: a public, demonstrative, and officially registered commitment to revolutionary values, which serves as evidence of past, an affirmation of present, and a promise of future activism on behalf of their respective partisan organizations.

The parallelism between the vanguard parties of Malevich and Lenin can be seen not only in the means by which they came to power, or their commitment to revolutionary partisanship. It extended even to such details as the name by which UNOVIS's supervisory body eventually came to be known.[41] The elected group that was headquartered at the People's School of Art and that made the decisions for both the art school and the art collective was initially called the Creative Committee (Tvorcheskii Komitet, or TvorKom for short), possibly on the model of the Vitebsk Revolutionary Committee (RevKom) to whom UNOVIS formally submitted a request for official recognition as an autonomous art organization.[42] However, this body soon changed its name to the Central Creative Committee (Tsentral'nyi TvorKom)[43]—a designation that echoed the abbreviated nomenclature used by the apparatus of both the Bolshevik Party (Tsentral'nyi Komitet, or TsK) and the Soviet state (Tsentral'nyi Isponitelnyi Komitet, or TsIK). Significantly, this new name was adopted immediately after UNOVIS launched a concerted campaign to expand its influence beyond the confines of the Vitebsk People's School of Art by establishing branches in other provincial cities. Nor did UNOVIS stop at national expansion. At the height of the prestige and power of the international Communist movement, in the fall of 1920, UNOVIS even created its very own International Bureau to publicize the tenets of Suprematism abroad.[44] It seems as though for Suprematism to supersede Communism, UNOVIS needed to adopt the same organizational structure and nomenclature as the institution that it hoped ultimately to replace.

The text of the statutes that UNOVIS submitted to the local authorities for the Vitebsk region in May 1920 provides further evidence of a kinship, albeit unidirectional, between the parties of Malevich and Lenin.[45] A close reading of the "Regulations of UNOVIS" reveals the extent to which the members of UNOVIS, and Malevich in particular, echoed the principles, and even the wording, detailed in the "Regulations (*ustav*) of the Russian Communist Party," which had been published just four months earlier, in January 1920. Malevich, who "undoubtedly took a leading role

Table 1. UNOVIS and Communist Party Regulations: A Comparison

UNOVIS Regulations	Regulations of the Russian Communist Party (Bolsheviks)
Party consists of members and candidate members.	The party consists of members and candidate members.
UNOVIS members "sympathize with its goals and are actively working to carry out the ideas of UNOVIS." Economic support consists of dues.	A party member is anyone who accepts the party program, works in one of its organizations, and pays membership dues.
Acceptance as a member of UNOVIS requires a majority of three-fourths of the votes of the Creative Committee (TK) and then is presented by the TK for support at the General Meeting.	New members are accepted by local party committees and are approved by the next General Meeting.
(1) The General Meeting and (2) the Creative Committee direct all matters of UNOVIS.	The General Meeting elects a committee which is the Executive Committee (TsIK) and directs all work of the local organization.
General Meetings occur according to necessity but not less than once every two weeks. A quorum for the general meeting is one-half of its members.	A Congress has a quorum if at least half of the party members are represented at it.
At the General Meeting candidates have a consulting vote.	Candidates may attend open general meetings of the party organization with a consultative vote.
At the head of UNOVIS is the Creative Committee (TK), which directs all activities of UNOVIS.*	The Congress is the highest organ of the party. The Congress elects the Central Committee (TsK).
The TK meetings occur according to necessity but not less than one time per week.	The TsK holds at least two plenums monthly.
UNOVIS has its own press, UNOVIS-Vitebsk.	Every party organization has the right to acquire its own press.

*UNOVIS reversed the relationship between party and Creative Committee so that the Creative Committee (TK) has control over the general party, thus assuring Malevich's leading role in UNOVIS.

in the formulation" of the UNOVIS Regulations, not only registered the autonomous art organization with the authorities (see table 1), but also did so using the language of Soviet officialdom itself.[46]

Significantly, although the members of the UNOVIS collective called themselves a "party," unlike the Bolsheviks they did not profess any explicit political program.[47] At a time when other independent organizations, clubs, and associations consisting primarily of prerevolutionary intellectuals were often construed by the authorities as possible sites of resistance, UNOVIS instead presented itself as an engaged, if unaffiliated, art group.[48] The UNOVIS members posed no political threat and actively sought to rebrand "Futurist" art by promoting a new, much more acceptable image of those in the vanguard—one in which modernist artists appeared not as the practitioners of some abstruse craft in possession of useless knowledge, but rather as highly qualified and indispensable specialists, who realized (in various media) the strategic vision of the party-state and molded (through various educational institutions) young Soviet minds, and who were, therefore, an integral part of the socialist project. From this perspective, even their self-effacement in the name of communal work—a black square in the place of a signature—can be seen as part of a careful attempt to counter the preconceptions of those local officials who believed that the intelligentsia was permeated with bourgeois individualists and who would undoubtedly have looked askance at this motley assortment of metropolitan modernists. Registration with the Vitebsk RevKom was thus not only a dutifully performed obligation, but also an attempt by the leaders of UNOVIS to present themselves as part of the Soviet public sphere (*obshchestvennost'*) rather than as holdovers of bourgeois civil society.[49]

The fate of a design that was supposed to decorate the side of the freight train carrying the Vitebsk faculty and students to a Moscow conference in June 1920 offers another example of the group's attention to the popular reception of its self-presentation, and its desire to fit into the discourses circulating within the Soviet public sphere. Originally, the train car was to bear the group's emblem, the black square, "underneath which was the motto 'Long Live UNOVIS.'" However, as Shatskikh points out, "for the actual trip . . . it was replaced by a long transparency" (see figures 5 and 6) identifying the passengers as "A group of travelers from the Vitebsk Free State Arts Studios who will participate in the All-Russian Conference of Art Schools."[50] The planned use of the slogan "Long Live UNOVIS" (*Da zdravstvuet UNOVIS*) clearly mirrored the frequent and enthusiastic use of the term "*Da zdravstvuet*" in Soviet propaganda posters, such as in S. Ivanov's 1920 poster *Long Live the Third Communist International!* (*Da zdravstvuet III kommunisticheskii internatsional'!*; see figure 7). This poster, along with other forms of Communist propaganda, was distributed via specially designated "Agitational Trains," which crisscrossed the Soviet Union and brought the regime's message to the countryside.[51] Apparently, the UNOVIS "agit-train" was meant to carry an equally partisan slogan. However, the members of UNOVIS ultimately decided on something that was more explanatory rather than exclamatory—a move that can be seen as

Figure 5. Nikolai Suetin, *Drawing for Wagon with UNOVIS Symbol for the Train Trip to Moscow*. 1920. Paper, gouache, watercolor, and tusche. 20.3 × 18.2 cm. State Russian Museum. Copyright © 2012 Artists Rights Society (ARS), New York/ VG Bild-Kunst, Bonn.

a way to confer legitimacy on the artists and students invited to the capital to participate in a state-sponsored conference without offending the sensibilities of the conference organizers and sponsors.

In keeping with its unaffiliated position, UNOVIS for the most part carefully avoided addressing political issues. In January 1921, however, just a few months before the start of the Eleventh Party Congress, Malevich published an article "About the Party in Art" in which he explicitly argued that the creation of the cultural framework of the future "should not be of a party character." He went on to say that the state should be concerned about political and economic sectors of life but that "all other areas should be nonparty, especially art."[52] This was one of Malevich's clearest avowals of the necessity to maintain art as a discrete sphere of activity in Soviet society, and its programmatic nature is apparent from the fact that this oracular pronouncement appeared in an article that opened the second issue of the *UNOVIS Almanac*, the official publication of the Vitebsk Suprematists. The same issue of the almanac also included a piece on "The Party Spirit [*partiinost'*] in Art," which was written by Moisei Kunin (1897–1972), a student of Malevich at the Vitebsk People's School of Art. Kunin initially argued that the concepts of "art" and "party" were mutually exclusive, but then went on to suggest that UNOVIS itself was a cohesive party, "creating a new world . . . in accordance with the new forms of the commune."[53]

Figure 6. Unknown photographer, teachers and students of UNOVIS in Vitebsk, before their departure for Moscow to participate in the All-Russia Conference of Art Teachers and Students. June 1920.

Both of these essays have been interpreted as clear statements opposing increased Communist Party control over artistic activity.[54] And indeed, Kunin's concept of "party" describes an independent organization devoted to "the emancipation of art" and is clearly not that espoused by the Bolsheviks. But calling for cultural autonomy from the party-state did not mean that Malevich and his followers were willing to abandon the partisan nature

Figure 7. Sergei Ivanov, *Long Live the Third Communist International!* 1920. Colored lithograph. 66 × 88 cm. Slavic and Baltic Division, New York Public Library, Astor, Lenox, and Tilden Foundations.

of its revolutionary artistic activity in favor of cultural pluralism. On the contrary, if anything, this was a call to let UNOVIS do in art what the Communist Party was doing in other fields of Soviet life, namely, to monopolize both the agenda and the means to carry it out.

The UNOVIS Brand

In addition to setting up a curriculum focused on teaching "cubism, futurism, Suprematism, and collective creativity in that area," the group of artists around Malevich promoted a "new utilitarian world of things" and applied Suprematist visual language to the design of such elements of everyday Soviet life (*byt*) as ration cards, signboards, and public festival decorations.[55] Indeed, as the 1920 program of the aforementioned Central Creative Committee (Tsentral'nyi TvorKom) attests, UNOVIS members repeatedly stressed the utilitarian application of their abstract style and actively sought to position themselves as not only an indispensable element of the nascent Soviet public sphere but also as the sole arbiters of what constituted genuinely Soviet modernist art.[56] By setting itself up as an autonomous artistic organization whose primary function was the task of carrying out the "creation of furniture and all objects of practical use," as well as "designs of monumental decoration for use in the national holidays," UNOVIS became not only the artistic seal of quality, but also an early Soviet brand name.[57] Even if the utilitarian orientation of Suprematism was El Lissitzky's contribution to UNOVIS, as Aleksandra Shatskikh argues, the fact that Malevich embraced this trend and incorporated it into both the basic premise of UNOVIS and his pedagogical activity demonstrates his clear interest in creating and marketing UNOVIS's brand of sovietized abstract art. Malevich's letter to fellow UNOVIS member Ivan Kudryashev demonstrates Malevich's plans for literally constructing a socialist town out of Suprematist forms, including an economic-agricultural/agronomic center, fields, roads, a train station, an airplane, and a port that "we are building to preserve the Suprematist view and dynamism of form."[58]

In the course of soliciting important government commissions, Malevich publicly touted UNOVIS as the bridge between the "new spiritual and utilitarian world" and tirelessly promoted himself and his colleagues as "necessary specialists" for the Soviet republic, who alone among all the existing art groups would be solely responsible for creating the material reality of this new world.[59] Using the militaristic discourse that had come to dominate civilian life in the aftermath of the Civil War, and that was espoused by the Leon Trotsky and the proponents of War Communism, Malevich described UNOVIS as an "army of the new art . . . All utilitarian objects of the new life, a new city, new painting, new music, new theater, should be created by this army."[60] Like any successful military leader, Malevich led his troops by example. For instance, even before the formal constitution of UNOVIS, Malevich had sought out the Vitebsk commissar of the arts (Chagall), who was charged with finding artists to execute designs for public decorations to celebrate official state holidays and events. In short order, Malevich was assigned the task of serving as head of the decoration committee for the second anniversary of the founding of the Committee for the Struggle Against Unemployment (Komitet po bor'be s bezrabotitsei). Along with El Lissitzky and a group of enthusiastic People's School of Art students, Malevich planned and executed the decoration of the building in which this organization was located, strewing the surrounding streets of the city with Suprematist banners. Lissitzky, Malevich's second-in-command, also designed the cover of a booklet titled *Committee for the Struggle Against Unemployment*, which was published in Vitebsk in 1919.[61]

In February 1920, soon after the artists who had coalesced around Malevich founded UNOVIS, they were tapped to participate in the decoration of Vitebsk for "Front Week." Whereas modernist artists had been banned from contributing decorations for Moscow and Petrograd public celebrations, Malevich and his followers had free rein in Vitebsk, and the city was quickly covered with geometric shapes and bright colors.[62] For example, David Yakerson (1896–1947) designed a Suprematist base for a monument to Karl Marx,[63] which in some ways prefigured Malevich's later concept for a bust honoring the assassinated Communist Party leader Sergei Kirov.[64] Malevich himself created a speaker's rostrum (tribune) that was decorated with Suprematist symbols and inscribed with the slogan: "Labor, Knowledge, and Art—The Basis of a Communist Society."[65] However, of all the practical applications of Suprematism, the abstract, geometric paintings in El Lissitzky's PROUN series came closest to realizing UNOVIS's goal of reinventing the world according to Suprematist tenets. PROUN should be read as a contraction of the term "designed by UNOVIS" (proekt UNOVISA) or "Design for the Affirmation of the New" (Proekt utverzhdeniia novogo).[66] As Shatskikh details, Lissitzky's PROUN series gave rise to several Suprematist projects in various media. This included not only posters, such as Lissitzky's famous *Beat the Whites with the Red Wedge* from early 1920, in which the epic battle between Red and White forces is allegorized by geometric abstractions in red, white, and black; but also architectural designs like the "Lenin Tribune," a speaker's rostrum conceived out of concrete geometric forms.

Production Propaganda

Marketing the UNOVIS brand, however, was only the first step in a campaign to solidify the position of the leadership of the People's School of Art. Successfully inserting UNOVIS into the Soviet public sphere entailed first articulating and then demonstrating precisely how Suprematism, and the modernist artists who espoused it, could be useful to the Soviet state. And by embracing the general enthusiasm for technology, especially its role in expanding industrial production and manufacturing, Malevich, his colleagues, and their students attempted to do just that. We must not forget that the administrators of this state-funded educational institution were accountable to central and local authorities. And ever since the founding of the Soviet republic, those authorities were preoccupied with industry and technology as the key to the creation of a modern industrialized state.[67] Bolshevik enthusiasm about the promise of industrial technology and production occupied a prominent place in the party agenda. The 1919 party program, for example, stressed the "increase of productive forces of the country" as "the fundamental and principal point upon which the economic policy of the Soviet government is based."[68] The Ninth Congress of the Russian Communist Party (Bolsheviks), which took place in late March 1920, also placed economic development through industry at the top of the agenda and detailed the urgent plans to be implemented to increase production.[69] In May 1920 the journal *Public Education* (*Narodnoe prosveshchenie*), the official organ of the Soviet Commissariat of Enlightenment, published a similar appeal, thereby demonstrating the agency's commitment to the task of mobilizing the cultural and educational institutions under its jurisdiction, including those responsible for the administration of art schools throughout the country, in the effort to raise the level of production and industry.[70]

This activity was all part of what came to be known as "production propaganda," a policy that at the time was seen as vital to the country's postwar economic recovery as the New Economic Policy. Although "production propaganda" affected education, publication policy, arts policy, and production, it has been almost entirely ignored by scholars outside Russia, and so merits a brief description.[71] The purpose of this policy was the wide-scale popularization of technological, industrial, and manufacturing processes among the urban and provincial proletariat, in a coordinated effort to increase workers' consciousness about methods of socialist construction. Production propaganda conflated economic and ideological discourses, since workers were to be trained to understand the "organic connection between separate parts of the economy" and how their participation would aid in the development of the RSFSR on the foundations of Communism.[72] Nadezhda Krupskaya envisioned production propaganda as a means of creating the "psychological precondition for socialist production."[73] Lenin's own "Theses on Production Propaganda," written in November 1920, argued that this policy must be "given special prominence." He insisted that "the leading newspapers Izvestiya and Pravda should reduce space devoted to politics and increase the space for production propaganda."[74] Lenin's exhortation seemed to have the desired effect: between January and June 1921, over forty articles on the topic appeared in *Pravda* alone. But the creation of production propaganda did not stop with the publication of newspaper articles in the central newspapers. Across the country, party activists gave speeches about production plans and electrification in worker clubs; museum staff staged art exhibitions dedicated to factory life; musicians composed operas which praised heroic workers; and art departments in the center and in the provinces helped to organize and create posters for public festivities celebrating such events as "Days of Electrification" and "Days of Fuel."[75] Indeed, for the first few years after the Russian Civil War, the rhetoric of production and manufacturing appeared to infuse almost every aspect of public life in Soviet Russia.

As UNOVIS's own publications demonstrate, the collective in charge of the Vitebsk People's School of Art's administration was eager to advertise its contribution to this national effort. The second issue of the *UNOVIS Almanac,* for example, included at least two articles stressing the vanguard artists' role as engineers of production propaganda, both of them written by students working in the architecture studio run by Lissitzky. For example, in his essay "UNOVIS in the Studios," the Suprematist architect Lazar Khidekel (1904–1986) deliberately emphasized the objective approaches employed while "performing our analysis." He affirmed the emergent technological orientation of Soviet society as a whole by arguing that "in the equipping of the technico-electrical state, there is no place for the artist with his aesthetic rubbish ... In this work we must participate on an equal level with the engineer, the agronomist, and workers of all specialties."[76] Ilya Chashnik (1902–1929), a Moscow art student who accompanied Malevich to Vitebsk and who at the time was Khidekel's classmate, was "famous for his inexhaustible inventiveness and ability to apply Suprematist principles to virtually all forms of art"[77] and continued the utilitarian and technological themes in his essay on "The Architectural and Technical Faculty." He wrote about the importance of "working in unison with astronomers, engineers, and mechanics" and the necessity of "leading Suprematism out of its draughtsmanly, plan-making [stage] into the organisms of utilitarian forms for new objects" by means of "electric machines and ... the technology of magnetic forces ... for a unified aspiration to construct organisms of Suprematism."[78] By demonstrating their wholehearted enthusiasm for modern technology, especially its practical application to the task of expanding industrial production and manufacturing, these two young contributors to the *UNOVIS Almanac* presented themselves, and by extension the progressive art school in which they were educated and trained, as full-fledged members of the new, revolutionary, Soviet technical intelligentsia. A concrete example of Suprematism-inflected production propaganda is El Lissitzky's signboard (now lost) *Workbenches Await You* (see figure 8), which combines geometric forms with a slogan taken straight from the production propaganda campaign.[79]

Consistent with the art group's embrace of production and technology was UNOVIS's identity as a "scientific research institute ... engaged in practical work."[80] Loren Graham has described the establishment of the idea of the research institute as perhaps the most significant reform of science that the Soviet government enacted in the 1920s. In the Soviet Union the term "scientific-research institute" (*nauchno-issledovatel'skii institut*) carried a stature and a meaning that it did not have in any other country, especially in the capitalist West.[81] Already in 1919 and early 1920, research institutes devoted to biology, geology, and material culture had been established in the hopes that they would become Marxist outposts, which would lead the way in study and research based on Marxist methodology.[82] In the fall of 1920, an Institute of Scientific Methodology was even founded under the aegis of Narkompros,[83] a development that justified UNOVIS's self-characterization as laboratory researchers and that helps to explain, at

Figure 8. Unknown photographer, El Lissitzky, *Workbenches Await You.* 1920. Propaganda board, Vitebsk.

least in part, why Malevich began his career-long obsession with scientific research methods of data collection and the use of charts at the People's School of Art.

Malevich as a Model Soviet Professor

If the Vitebsk People's School of Art's art studios became "laboratories" of production propaganda for UNOVIS's "scientific researchers," then the school's classrooms were the group's testing ground as the first cohort of a distinctively modern Soviet art professoriate. As is well known, the genesis of UNOVIS coincided with changes in the administration of Soviet educational institutions and with Narkompros's increasing emphasis on practical and political education, as well as systematic and objective methods of teaching and research. And from the moment that it was articulated in the very first issue of the *UNOVIS Almanac,* the UNOVIS program definitely echoed these imperatives. The policies adopted by Ermolaeva and implemented by the faculty of the People's School of Art successfully united both of the major trends, or rather, competing priorities, that had emerged in the sphere of arts education by the middle of 1920: the commitment to training unprecedented numbers of students in the history and practice of fine arts, such as that exemplified by the system of Free Art Studios (SVOMAS); and the application of art and design to projects necessary for the Soviet state. UNOVIS's pedagogical policies, in turn, were informed by an educational program that was "systematic"—an important keyword in Soviet parlance—and oriented toward both the materialist worldview and the utilitarian application of the artistic approach pioneered by Malevich. As we will see, the *UNOVIS Almanac,* and the pedagogical model it proposes, allows us to trace a shift from the program that Malevich articulated for his studio in Moscow to that adopted by his studio in Vitebsk, a shift in which Suprematism is explicitly connected not only to utilitarian objects but also to a logical system to be explicated by the People's School of Art faculty. A comparison of these two programs allows us to witness, in other words, how Suprematism came to be reconceptualized as a specifically Soviet pedagogical modality to be put into practice by a new Soviet professoriate (see figure 9).

Not surprisingly, the effort to combine Suprematist theory and Soviet pedagogical practice can be seen most clearly in the case of Malevich himself. Although some of Malevich's prerevolutionary publications, most notably *From Cubism to Futurism and Suprematism* (1915), offer an explanation for the advent of Suprematism and its corresponding worldview, it is his postrevolutionary statements that make explicit a logical progression and a connection with world events that was only implicit in earlier published work.[84] For example, in the 1919 brochure accompanying the Tenth State Exhibition devoted to Suprematism and nonobjective art, Malevich wrote that "Suprematism is a definite system . . . a hard, cold, system, unsmilingly set in motion by philosophical thought."[85] This "systematic," philosophical approach to the history of art was spelled out most clearly in "On New Systems of Art" (1919), which positioned Suprematism and its founder as much more than a primus inter pares:

> Thus in constructing painterly forms, it is essential to have a system for their construction, a law for their constructional interrelationships. As soon as such a construction is built up, it will express a new physical conclusion and become objective, alongside the other painterly forms of the world.[86]

Figure 9. Unknown photographer, UNOVIS studio, Vitebsk, 1921.

The deterministic and teleological explanation outlined in Malevich's booklet, which, as we saw, was written in Moscow but published in Vitebsk, would ultimately be fleshed out and further refined in Petrograd as the "Theory of the Additional Element." But it is significant that this foundational Suprematist text was first published as a proselytizing and recruiting tool upon his arrival at the Vitebsk People's School of Art. For it allows us to see how adaptable and responsive Malevich's program could be to local needs, in this case, the need to create an audience for his teaching.

If we compare the pedagogical program that he wrote in 1919 for the Free Art Studios (SVOMAS) in Moscow with the one that he published just one year later for his primary audience in Vitebsk, we can see this flexibility in action. For example, in his 1919 program, Malevich had described the artistic trends that he taught as "Cubism, Futurism, and Suprematism—the new realism of a painterly worldview [*Weltanschauung*]." A student enrolled in his Moscow studio could expect to investigate different aspects of Suprematism, including "Form, Space, and Time" and "Color as Two-Dimensional Art." Nowhere in this document is there even a hint of any kind of practical application of Suprematism. Instead, this formulation merely reiterates earlier statements to the effect that his approach is the logical culmination of modernist artistic experimentation and the only mode to access the reality beyond the illusion of our three-dimensional world. The Vitebsk People's School of Art pedagogical program, on the other hand, makes explicit the "systematic" approach behind such rather vague and self-serving formulations. According to this document, students matriculating at the People's School of Art would first be immersed in techniques of abstraction (taught by Ermolaeva), then Cubism (taught by Kogan), and finally Suprematism (taught by Malevich himself). Malevich's definition of modernist art would thereby be presented not as an end in itself, as it was in the SVOMAS program, but rather as a rational and inevitable component of a larger system of historical development. Malevich's students in the Suprematism Division would be taught systems of construction, "Architecture: Three Dimensional Suprematism," "The Square—Its Economic Development," "Philosophy of Suprematism," "The Inner Development of Natural Science Constructions," and "The Collective as the Road to Unity."[87]

Furthermore, whereas the SVOMAS pedagogical program did not provide any room for the application of Suprematism to utilitarian objects, the People's School of Art program specifically mentions a "decorative studio" in which students are supposed to apply Suprematism to "theater, decorative compositions, murals, and the creation of objects."[88] As these examples demonstrate, during his stay in Vitebsk, Malevich's orientation shifted from the teaching of pure painting as an end in itself to a more utilitarian and systematic approach—one that, as Aleksandra Shatskikh points out, is akin to the pedagogical approach embraced by VKhUTEMAS, the more politically correct institutional successor to the State Free Art Studios.[89] In effect, comparing these two pedagogical programs allows us to follow Malevich's attempt to transform himself into a model Soviet professor, committed to adapting his abstract philosophy to, and participating in, the evolving discourse of Socialist construction.

The People's School of Art Under Attack

The case of Vitebsk in the early Soviet era presents scholars with a unique opportunity to hear the multiplicity of voices contributing to the often combative conversation about art in the new Soviet state. While there did seem to be a brief period, until about the end of 1920, when all artistic trends were visible and modernism was even the dominant mode of representation, by the winter of 1921, the voices expressing frustration with vanguard art and calling for a more representational type of art were beginning to drown out the voices of the modernists. This shift in artistic sensibilities and patronage patterns was not only a counterreaction to the "monopolistic" position held by UNOVIS, but also a direct result of the increasing pressure for ideological and political conformity that followed in the wake of the Eleventh Party Congress (1921), which reasserted the Leninist principle of "democratic centralism" and formulated a strategy of postwar reconstruction known as the New Economic Policy. Although from the perspective of Stalin's Great Break, the NEP period appeared as a time of relative creative freedom,[90] it is clear that standardization and regulation in the creative spheres and within the intelligentsia was not a deviation from, but an integral component of, the new party policy.[91]

This trend away from pluralism and toward homogeneity in the arts can also be observed in Vitebsk, and it can be traced on the pages of the art periodicals of the time. Thus, in the winter of 1921, Alexander Romm, by then a director of the regional sub-Department of Fine Arts within Narkompros, published an article-length diatribe against the People's School of Art[92] in which he expressed his frustration at the fact that "until now, the ruling group was UNOVIS: its dictatorship put its stamp on all pedagogical work of the studios." He observed that "students wishing to study Impressionism, Classicism, and Neoclassicism absolutely lacked the possibility to receive training," except in the two extreme trends of the "Naturalist academy [Pen's studio] or the academy of the 'Supremo-cubists.'" He then announced a fait accompli of great consequence for the members of the maligned "ruling group" of "Supremo-cubists": "The studios are inviting new teachers: Fal'k (Cezannist), Kuprin (Impressionist), as well as a new director of sculpting [David Yakerson, who had been in Vitebsk since 1919]," who was intended as a replacement for El Lissitzky, one of the main ideologists of the UNOVIS "dictatorship." Romm concluded on an optimistic note, saying that from now on, the "organization of these new studios will [lead to] normal pedagogical work of the studios."[93] This article is interesting for several reasons, not least of which is the light it sheds on the political scruples of its author, a modernist who had once served as head of the commission responsible for decorating Vitebsk for the first anniversary of the October Revolution, helped to found both the People's School of Art and the Vitebsk Museum of Art, and replaced Chagall as the director of the Museum and Regional sections of the Department of Fine Arts upon the latter's departure for Leningrad.[94] Precisely because this article was written by someone who had once been an influential member of the network of modernist artists who had resettled in Vitebsk, it reveals an internal fissure within the modernist camp itself.

While on the one hand Romm was calling for more pluralism, rather than less, it is also clear that he had little sympathy for the regnant paradigm at the Vitebsk People's School of Art. In his follow-up article, an exhibition review from August 1921, Romm described UNOVIS with even less sympathy than previously. "At the exhibition we expected to find some real achievements, concrete proofs of a fundamental understanding of the new painterly system." But instead, "what was on display were examples of Cubist painting." Romm's reaction to Lissitzky's designs for electric power-generating stations and a train station was short and damning: seeing this work, "the dilettantism of these architectural projects now becomes clear."[95] Were it not for the fact that Romm occupied an important position within the Soviet art bureaucracy, these mean-spirited characterizations might easily have been shrugged off as the carping of a jealous former colleague. But since *Art* (*Iskusstvo*), the journal in which Romm's two articles had appeared, was copublished by the Art Department of the Regional Administration of Political Education and RABIS, the trade union for artists, the plaintive voice of the jealous colleague automatically assumed the authoritative tone of the Soviet regime and was taken, not least by the author himself, to express the official, state-sanctioned view about art. And not entirely without reason. For although the editorial board of *Art* promised that it would "completely encompass artistic contemporaneity,"[96] and even published Malevich's piece about UNOVIS,[97] the combative tone of this "thick journal" was established in its very first issue, in an article written by none other than the commissar of enlightenment himself. Lunacharsky's essay, entitled "Art and Revolution," took particular aim at the modernists. "I come out against those who demand cultural break with past epochs," he wrote. "This is not a Marxist concept but [an] anarchist [one]." While claiming the modernist poet Vladimir Mayakovsky as an artist who was "close to us," he admonished the modernists for their "art of 'pure form' (without content)" that "leads to the creation of nonorganic forms (Cubism,

Suprematism, etc.)." After describing art's potential in furthering the revolution, a basic tenet of Soviet policy, Lunacharsky proclaimed: "This is why an authentic artist cannot be apolitical. He should be a true communist." The commissar of enlightenment concluded his essay by specifying that "the new art should be without roguishness or darkness, but *bright, convincing, generally accessible*," in other words, everything that "Futurism" was not, at least in his presentation.[98]

The second issue of *Art* included yet another critical piece by Romm. Although this article was ostensibly "About Museum Construction and the Vitebsk Museum of Contemporary Art," in reality, it was another not-so-subtle attack on the Suprematist leadership of the recently renamed Vitebsk Art-Practical Institute. Romm described the founding principles of the new type of museum and chronicled the difficult conditions under which it had to operate. He also noted that twelve months after its opening, the Vitebsk museum was still forced to share space with the art school. Although local officials apparently made a "categorical pronouncement" that the existence of the museum was harmful for the academic work of the art school and resolved to find alternative accommodations, by March 1921, the time of publication of Romm's article, the search for new quarters had not yet been completed. The head of the museum section of the Department of Fine Arts concluded his article by declaring that the "museum, so necessary to Vitebsk, cannot be and should not remain [hidden] 'under a bushel'" and by promising that in the "near future the question . . . about the accommodations of the museum [will finally be] resolved."[99] Coming from the pen of one of the most vocal critics of UNOVIS, this vow to "resolve" the situation at 10 Bukharin Street boded ill for the leadership of the People's School of Art.

But an even more alarming development was the unexpected defection of Kunin, one of UNOVIS's own members. As we saw, Kunin was a student in the UNOVIS studios and had contributed to the *UNOVIS Almanac.* However, the article that he published in the second issue of *Art* constituted nothing less than a public break with the UNOVIS network and its platform. Kunin began his piece "About UNOVIS" with a confession: "The more I was at their displays, the more everything became more and more muddled." But the "reason for this" confusion was not his own lack of faith in the charisma of his former teacher, but rather "the absence of a definite program." After describing the People's School of Art's origins and basic curriculum, Kunin went on the offensive. He sharply criticized Malevich for "negating painterly culture" and promoting instead an "illogical transition from painting to technology." He sarcastically remarked: "So Artists, lay down your instruments, don't do anything else except take up technology."

Kunin castigated Malevich not only for exhausting Suprematism, but also for inappropriately applying Suprematism to tribunes and posters:

> But when the whole city was dressed in squares, circles and triangles, it became terribly wild, absurd and silly, and clearly Suprematism in this area could not be fostered. Then Suprematism found its application in theater. Suprematist decorations, Suprematist ballet. But here also the . . . adoption of Suprematism did not meet with success. The experience of . . . "Victory over the Sun" sufficiently showed that Suprematism has no place in theater. Malevich sees that there is nothing for him to do on earth and goes to the heavens. He wants to decorate space. Your idea, comrade Malevich, would be somewhat valuable . . . several centuries ago. But now (to fly across the Atlantic in 15 hours) it is a little late. . . . Tell me where are your projects? There are none and will be none. And architecture in Suprematism did not manage to make anything. UNOVIS negates all painterly culture; UNOVIS negates authentic theater, poetry, music, and all types of art . . . From all the above stated it follows that UNOVIS should not be a place to study the culture of painting . . . we want authentic painterly culture . . . we are against circles squares triangles and nonsensical words about the building of a mobile station in space.[100]

This vitriolic diatribe deserves to be quoted at such length because for all their hyperbole, Kunin's observations actually strike at the heart of Malevich's strategy for making Suprematism Soviet. By presenting UNOVIS's enthusiastic embrace of technology and the application of Suprematism to propaganda as the very reason for its dramatic failure, the disgruntled student publicly mocked the tenets espoused by his teachers at the People's School of Art, thus joining Romm and the increasingly loud chorus of voices of opposition to Malevich's "party" and its peculiar brand of modernism.

Despite these setbacks, the work of modern artists affiliated with the UNOVIS collective continued to go on display, both at the school and at the Vitebsk Museum of Painterly Culture and at temporary art installations around town. In the previously mentioned review article from the second issue of *Art,* Romm offered a brief summary of this sporadic exhibition activity on the part of UNOVIS, if only to question its value. "Although Vitebsk has lately become a significant artistic center, and although Chagall, Dobuzhinsky, Puni, Malevich, and Fal'k [once] worked here, the accessibility of art for the masses has not been achieved." According to Romm, due to the increasingly "difficult conditions of life" in the region, which had only recently served as a battleground during the Russo-Polish War of 1920–

21,[101] no exhibitions at all had been staged since the big 1919 exhibition that represented local and Moscow artists. However, Romm reported, in the last few months of the spring and summer of 1921, four new exhibitions had been mounted and a few more were being planned by the "Group of Three." This group consisted of three young apprentices from the People's School of Art studios: E. B.Volkhonsky (active 1919),[102] Lev Yakovlevich Zevin (1902–1942),[103] and Kunin, whose work Romm compared favorably with that of Shterenberg and even Kandinsky. According to Romm, all three artists were studying Paul Cézanne's work and formulating the "beginning of painterly culture in the purest sense."[104] More importantly, their work was completely disassociated from the "ideology of the once all-powerful UNOVIS." So even though the "Group of Three" exhibition was carried out "under inauspicious conditions"—only three days in a cafeteria of the building on Bukharin Street—that at least was better than the UNOVIS exhibition, which was only open for one day. For critics of the Malevich "party," even such small victories were occasions for public celebration.

The Vitebsk Art-Practical Institute

The attack on the pedagogical practices of UNOVIS must be seen in the context of the postwar shift in educational policy, which became more hostile to the kind of progressive training offered at the Vitebsk People's School of Art and emboldened critics like Romm and Kunin. But the large temporal gap between the publication of a Soviet decree for a particular policy and its realization, which we noted in our discussion of the Moscow Museum of Painterly Culture, was even wider in the provinces. Consequently, in February 1921, several months after the reorganization of the Commissariat of Enlightenment, the People's School of Art studios were still operating under what remained of the Department of Fine Arts (IZO) and still receiving funds directly from Narkompros.[105] It was only in April 1921, a full six months after the reorganization was announced, that David Shterenberg, the new head of the Art Education Department of the Regional Administration of Professional Education, informed all provincial art departments that schools dedicated to training artists (musicians, writers, filmmakers, actors) were now formally administered by his agency, and that their current task was to provide professional training.[106] Mikhail Preobrazhensky, formerly a high-ranking Narkompros official, and now the head of the Main Administration of Professional Education, offered further clarification: while his agency would continue to support practicing artists, musicians, and writers, from now on its new focus would be on training art teachers who could be prepared to teach in schools around the country.

Preobrazhensky justified this shift in policy by the need to standardize all art education to better correspond "with the transition to a socialist structure" and to more firmly establish programs that would attract the "proletariat to all types of general and professional education."[107]

The Vitebsk People's School of Art was renamed the Vitebsk Art-Practical Institute when it was formally put under the jurisdiction of the Art Department of the Regional Department of Professional Education in April 1921.[108] This name change not only reflected the orientation of the Main Administration of Professional Education, but also underlined that the Vitebsk Art-Practical Institute was just another "institution of higher education" (*vysshee uchebnoe zavedenie*, or *VUZ*). As such, the art school was bound to conform to standard policies that applied to all the institutes and colleges across the country. Ermolaeva was thus faced with the task of reorienting the school's pedagogical program, including Malevich's UNOVIS studio, to accommodate the standards of professional education and practical training. The academic year, however, was almost over by the time the new administrative changes took effect. As a result, radical changes in the school's program and curriculum were not put into effect until the fall of 1921. However, one change was noticeable that spring and summer: a more consistent flow of funds and materials into the school. Rather than competing with every cultural-educational organization in the country for Narkompros's money, local institutions now petitioned their regional department of the Department of Professional Education, headed up by David Shterenberg, which had been infused with cash after the Narkompros reorganization of November 1920. Payment records from the art studios for winter and spring of 1921 reveal that instructors were receiving biweekly salaries of 9,335 rubles; and staff (such as librarians and bookkeepers) were paid between 2,000 and 6,000 rubles.[109] Occasionally everyone would receive double salaries as adjustments for inflation. By May, each faculty member was receiving 216,531 rubles per month.[110] Judging by the catastrophic financial situation faced by other teachers in the Vitebsk region, Shterenberg's attempt to sweeten the deal must have been gratefully accepted by the Vitebsk Art-Practical Institute administration.[111]

Inevitably, after the carrot, came the stick. In September 1921, Narkompros unveiled a plan for cutbacks in the number of institutes and colleges for the current academic year. Narkompros stipulated that the scaling-back of these academic institutions was to "be carried out only on a minimal scale" due to their importance for training new professionals.[112] However, some professionals were more important than others. In carrying out this policy, the Main Administration of Professional Education took particular aim at art schools: "In the interest of increasing higher professional education . . .

the network of [schools] should be increased in the areas of industry and medical education and scaled back in the area of artistic education."[113] The opinion that art institutions were of far less value for Soviet economic development was reflected in an early 1922 report in which Narkompros rated various colleges and institutes according to their perceived importance. We do not have the ranking for the Vitebsk Art-Practical Institute, but one of its peer institutions, Moscow's newly formed Higher Artistic-Technical Studios (Vysshie gosudarstvennye khudozhestvenno-tekhnichisskie masterskie, or VKhUTEMAS), which was also dominated by modernists, was ranked as having the very least importance out of sixteen institutions by Narkompros, and the least importance of nineteen institutions as ranked by the All-Union Council on the National Economy. Predictably, electronics and engineering institutes ranked highest.[114] In the words of Viktor Korablev, an art critic for *The Life of Art,* the Soviet state was "no longer in any condition to spend crazy amounts of money on often risky undertakings," such as the art schools that had "sprouted like mushrooms after a good rain" in the first years of Bolshevik rule, only to wither in the strapped financial climate of the immediate postwar period. "In the beginning of 1922 in Petrograd," Korablev noted, "there were only 17 art schools [left]: nine for music, two for drama, two for choreography, and four for fine art."[115] Archival research confirms this grim assessment: in 1920 and 1921 there were 176 institutes of fine art with 15,056 students. By 1922, 74 art institutes with 9,662 students remained on the state's payroll. In one year's time, 59 percent of fine art institutes and 82 percent of museums had closed their doors.[116]

Between January and May 1922, one-half of the cultural-educational institutions in the Vitebsk district were closed.[117] The sparse available funds were redirected toward the construction of reading rooms dedicated to "communist and agricultural propaganda."[118] The March report about the activity of the Vitebsk Department of Professional Education noted that within the art subdepartment, only two institutes remained open: the Vitebsk Conservatory and the Art-Practical Institute.[119] Furthermore, to improve the financial situation of the remaining schools, the Department of Professional Education adopted a "sink or swim" policy that was typical during the NEP era: those institutions which could not survive on their own would be shut down. The agency announced that from now on, students attending art colleges and institutes would be required to pay their own tuition, rather than rely on the state to subsidize their education.[120] This situation was a double-edged sword for art schools: their revenues could potentially increase, or they could lose the students and risk closure. The Council of People's Commissars (Sovnarkom) justified these closures by the fact that there was an "insufficient" number of students to begin with; that many of these educational institutions were near major centers with similar facilities; that they lacked professional personnel; and that they evinced what was euphemistically termed an "absence of sufficient depth in academic and practical preparation of workers."[121]

As we will see, the fact that the Vitebsk Art-Practical Institute survived this vicious round of school closures can be attributed, at least in part, to its administration's savvy curriculum adjustments, as a result of which the school became a "model" institute that conformed to the standards of art education as decreed by the Professional Education Department. However, one must also acknowledge the role played by the head of the Art Department, who formally supervised and presided over this massive cutback in the number of art institutions.[122] Shterenberg was himself part of the original network of modernists employed by the state within IZO, and he undoubtedly did what he could to make sure that his colleagues and friends were not left out in the cold. Judging by the synopsis of the September 1921 report about the activity of his department, Shterenberg exercised his personal influence to soften the hard line taken by his superiors in the Main Administration of Professional Education. At first glance, his synopsis that was published in the Administration of Professional Education's *Bulletin* appeared merely to restate official government policy. But a careful reading revealed a moderate approach. Shterenberg reiterated "that the practice of art as a means of relaxation should be abandoned." At the same time, he added, "It is necessary to recognize that production is impossible without participation of art and artistic education . . . and is an urgent task, like other branches of professional education." Deftly sidestepping the issue of school closures, he argued that "professional art schools should be in closest dependence with technology . . . and should be built upon production bases with strict planned tasks, arising from the demands of the last decade." And finally, what can be taken as a pointed rejoinder to the critics of modernism, he emphasized that "*all* trends in art [my emphasis] should be used for technical training of art students in art schools."[123] Clearly, how Soviet policy was implemented, and who was charged with implementing it, really mattered.

Shterenberg's agile political maneuvering on behalf of his modernist colleagues not only shielded them, but also served as a model for how to get things done. The plan for the new academic year, which Ermolaeva submitted to the Main Administration of Professional Education in September 1921, offers a perfect example of the way that the rector of the Vitebsk Art-Practical Institute interpreted the government's new expectations. It also demonstrates how cleverly she and the faculty had adapted the school's progressive curriculum to reflect the state-sponsored demands for higher standards of professional art education: practical orientation, the integration of social science, and clear guidelines for completing the course and earning a diploma. To convey the extent of these curriculum adjustments, I will quote at length from this previously unpublished document:

> The Vitebsk State Artistic-Practical Studios Academy is sending you its academic plan, supported by [the Central Professional Education Administration]. Study begins September 1, except for Professor Fal'k who has not yet arrived. The teachers are divided into two groups: 1) the Practical Division: Yu. Pen (painter) and D. A. Yakerson (sculptor) and 2) Research Division: K. S. Malevich, V. M. Ermolaeva, R. Fal'k, N. Kogan and G. Noskov. Courses will be given on mathematics, general science and . . . on art. The studios [also] have two parallel divisions: practical and academic research. The first has as its goal the preparation of researchers and innovators in the area of art; the second prepares masters-artists to fulfill tasks of the state—such as posters, portraits, sculptures, illustrations, and other agitational needs. Duration of study: four–five years. Goal: Preparation for teaching school. Division of Research Subjects: Systems of Cezanne, reconstruction, painterly constructions, spatial constructions; systems of dynamism, systems of speed; algebra, trigonometry, physics, astronomy; theory of painting, philosophy of painting, history of art; logic, psychology, social science, sociology, economics, politics; carpentry, metalwork, color chemistry. Fourth year: practical work. Division of Practical Painting and Sculpture: drawing, painting, sculpture, Constructivist drawing; history of art, history of posters; anatomy, logic, psychology, history; chemistry of colors, graphics.[124]

It is clear from this academic plan that Ermolaeva attempted to correlate the school's program with the Professional Education Department's demand that art training have a "practical" character, that graduates be adequately trained to take up posts in academies; and that they work to fulfill state commissions. It even took into account Lenin's dictum that history and political literacy be taught in all schools. Furthermore, unlike other institutes and colleges, the Vitebsk Art-Practical Institute met *all* the criteria outlined by the country's highest governing body: there were a sufficient number of students, there was no major city nearby with similar facilities; despite their associations with "Futurism," the staff was composed of professional artists; and there was evidence of "sufficient depth in academic and practical preparation of workers" in the academic plan. Artists associated with "left" art, such as Malevich and even Fal'k (who as a member of the Jack of Diamonds group was also associated with the lefts), had sequestered themselves in the "research division" so as not to appear to be training young art students in abstract art. Meanwhile, Pen, the academic realist, and Yakerson, the sculptor, were placed in charge of teaching basic art techniques. Most tellingly, no mention was made of UNOVIS or Suprematism.

The Vitebsk State Technicum

As the 1921–22 curriculum testifies, the rector, the professors, and the students at the Vitebsk Art-Practical Institute formally presented themselves as a united collective in service to the Soviet state. But they did so on "the terms of the new order," not that of UNOVIS.[125] Furthermore, even though the school survived this round of closures, Ermolaeva's request for additional credit, which was included with the academic plan sent to the Professional Education Department, went unfulfilled. So when the school year began, utility bills and salaries remained unpaid. And they continued to be so for the remainder of Ermolaeva's administration.

The school's vibrant pedagogical activities proceeded apace that year; however we know little of UNOVIS's activities during its last year in Vitebsk. The sparse facts are that in the winter of 1922, Malevich sought to establish a branch of UNOVIS in the Moscow Institute of Artistic Culture (INKhUK), but opposing theoretical views held by Malevich and the Moscow Constructivists made cooperation untenable.[126] UNOVIS members participated in an exhibition of provincial art schools in Moscow in March 1922, and another small exhibition was held in Vitebsk in May 1922.[127] UNOVIS probably did function in the "research" department of the school, inasmuch as it was able without funding or supplies, but there is little evidence that its activity rivaled that of the previous years. In addition, an increased amount of attention to potentially suspicious organizations, particularly "anti-Soviet groups among the intelligentsia," precipitated the reregistration of all groups and brought UNOVIS under closer scrutiny. As a self-styled member of the new Soviet professoriate, Malevich avoided the fate of some of his colleagues in other Soviet colleges and institutes, that of arrest and deportation.[128] Nevertheless, Malevich saw the writing on the wall. This, plus his wife's worsening health, prompted him to revisit his original plan of moving to Petrograd.

We know neither the precise circumstances nor the exact dates that Malevich, Ermolaeva, Kogan, and their students left Vitebsk. My research has revealed a number of divergent accounts of this "exodus." The extent to which UNOVIS was "forced out by local authorities" is debatable, as no archival evidence, to my knowledge, supports this claim.[129] Rather than being forced out by a single decree, Malevich, Ermolaeva, and their followers most likely left due to a host of other weighty reasons, not least of which was the steadily mounting criticism of this nest of modernist experimentation. But the worsening material conditions in Vitebsk figured perhaps even more prominently in their decision to depart. While in 1919 Vitebsk was an oasis of food and consumer goods, by 1921 the city was feeling the impact of the famine in the nearby Povolzh'e district. The teachers in the art school were going hungry due to the lack of food and financial support.[130] The final straw, however, was the imminent graduation and dispersal of Malevich's students, who constituted the bulk of the UNOVIS "party," and who provided the raison d'être for his studio at the Vitebsk Art-Practical Institute. With the students gone, and the studio empty, the UNOVIS network could no longer provide either the support or the security that Malevich expected. Consequently, with the graduation of ten students from the Vitebsk Art-Practical Institute in May 1922, UNOVIS effectively ceased to operate in Vitebsk.[131]

On May 22, 1922, Ermolaeva contacted the Petrograd Museum of Painterly Culture insisting that the paintings that were brought to Vitebsk for the museum "must be transferred from Vitebsk to a greater cultural center where they can be preserved" since with "the recent move of the faculty of the art school to Petrograd their destruction is inevitable."[132] Apparently at least some of the staff, most likely Fal'k and Malevich, had already left Vitebsk in May. Ermolaeva followed in August. All institute graduates except for Nina Kogan followed Malevich to Petrograd,[133] thus preserving the network. Then in late June she, too, wrote a letter to Mikhail Glibenko, the head of the Main Administration of Scientific, Scholarly-Artistic, and Museum Institutions, in which she described herself as a "specialist in the history of new left art and the explanation of it to the general masses" and requested a position in the Petrograd Museum of Painterly Culture as an excursion leader, thereby rejoining the modernist network that had been established there. Kogan's contract revealed that she was hired as an excursion leader and allowed to live in a Narkompros dormitory for free. In the spirit of NEP, her salary was one-half of the excursion fees.[134] According to archival documents, all the teachers and students associated with UNOVIS—save Ivan Gavris—had left for Petrograd by August 1922, and had established themselves in the Petrograd Museum of Painterly Culture. But as we will see in Chapter Three, the pedagogical principles and commitment to the application of abstraction to utilitarian purposes that they had developed during their residence in Vitebsk continued to inform their activity even after the disbanding of the UNOVIS group, and indeed, formed the basis of Malevich's pedagogical charts and systematic approach to the study and the creation of art.

Most scholarly accounts of the Vitebsk Art-Practical Institute end with the departure of Malevich and Ermolaeva, as if UNOVIS was synonymous with the institution as a whole—an interpretation originally propagated by contemporaries on both sides of the political fence that remains current until today.[135] However, tracing the development of this progressive art school over the next and final year of its existence is of interest because it lends further support to the argument that personal networks and patron-client relationships with highly placed Soviet bureaucrats were as crucial in deciding the fate of modernism during the NEP period as the changed ideological climate. Indeed, the last days of the Vitebsk Art-Practical Institute offer a particularly instructive example of the futility of going it alone. Although almost all the artists—save Ivan Gavris—associated with Suprematism had left Vitebsk, the Vitebsk Art-Practical Institute appears to have remained associated with Futurism and Suprematism in the minds of local art department officials, because the school continued to be unfunded for the remainder of 1922. The Collegium of the Vitebsk branch of the Administration for Regional Education eventually decided that it would be more efficient if the two remaining institutes would share the same space, so the first floor of the Institute was given to the Vitebsk Conservatory, thereby taking away one-half of the Vitebsk Art-Practical Institute's studio space.[136] According to a 1923 report filed by Ivan Gavris (1890–1937), a former modernist art student in the school, who replaced Ermolaeva as rector of the institute on August 15, 1922,[137] the Vitebsk Art-Practical Institute was refused funds and support in the fall of 1922, and consequently was "forced to give up those accommodations as a condition for funds."[138] Due to the sparse funds and loss of accommodations, Gavris was forced to close the carpentry, sculpture, and UNOVIS studios, as well as the museum. After the conservatory took over the first floor, the Vitebsk Art-Practical Institute was left with a total of three rooms for studios, which could only accommodate sixty students, and a small lecture hall. Despite the loss of one entire floor, the Vitebsk Art-Practical Institute was able to mount a "Survey Exhibition of the Vitebsk Art-Practical Institute" in May 1923. In a positive review of the exhibition, published in the *Vitebsk News* (*Vitebskie izvestiia*), the author (most likely Gavris himself) remarked on the "altogether difficult conditions, absence of materials and funds, and weak or completely unprepared teachers." "In the future," he continued, "the program of work of the institute will change to a more practical type" and specified that the Vitebsk Art-Practical Institute would take up the "important question of industrial arts and printing."[139]

But there would not be much of a future. In June 1923, Gavris was informed that the school would once again be relocated, this time to the currently unoccupied synagogue on Volodarsky Street. This move involved not only a physical relocation of the institute, but also its reorganization into a "technicum," defined in the *Narkompros Weekly* as an educational institution whose chief purpose was to "prepare teachers in all areas of work."[140] This meant that the scope of the training offered by the Vitebsk Art-Practical Institute would be narrowed significantly and artists would no longer be trained for a variety of artistic tasks, as they had been in the Art-Practical Institute, but only as art teachers. In a complaint addressed to the Pedagogical Council of the Regional Administration of Professional Education in fall 1922, the young rector vociferously objected to this high-handed and peremptory action, writing that moving the institute was "equal to the liquidation of the art school and art education in Vitebsk." In August Gavris also wrote to Shterenberg, still the head of the Art Department of the Main Administration of Professional Education, stating that the move to the synagogue was analogous to the closing of the institute.[141] But Shterenberg was no longer able to help. Gavris's adamant refusal to relocate the school prompted the Regional Administration of Professional Education to fire him effective as of August 1, thus removing the last vanguard artist from the former modernist stronghold. The Pedagogical Council protested the firing of Gavris and the nomination of a certain Tarasov as the temporary director, especially since the latter had "nothing in common with the matter of art and is undoubtedly negatively disposed to the situation of the school."[142] However, nobody paid attention to this protest and the reorganization and relocation proceeded as decreed.

As of September 1923, the new Vitebsk State Technicum was in the former synagogue, under the direction of sculptor Mikhail Kerzin (1883–1979), whose qualification for the job seems to have been that he was an administrator in the Art Workers' Union.[143] Of the former faculty, only Pen, Yudovin, Brazer, and Efim Minin (1897–1940), another of Pen's pupils, remained on as teachers. However, although none of them was affiliated with either Futurism or UNOVIS, they continued to take pride in the progressive, if not revolutionary, art school where they used to teach. As Minin recalled in his August 1923 report to the "Liquidation Commission"—the administrative body that handled closing of institutions—of the Worker-Peasant Inspectorate, during its heyday the Vitebsk Art-Practical Institute was "a center of artistic life" that "attracted artistic pioneers" and that "remained extant when many schools in the region were closed during NEP." He was either not aware of, or would not admit, the possibility that this art school managed to stay open as long as it did in part precisely because of its revolutionary nature, and the "experimental work by artist Chagall in the area of new painting, [and] by Malevich and Ermolaeva in the area of Supremo-architecture and nonobjective painting."[144] But as this chapter has argued, the school that is still associated with UNOVIS—closely tied with the shifts in Bolshevik political and economic policy and, to a great extent, shaped in response to those policies—is an excellent case study of a self-conscious and remarkably successful transformation of a bastion of vanguard modernism into a model Soviet institute of higher learning.

Chapter Three

The Last Citadel: The Petrograd Museum of Artistic Culture and GINKhUK, 1919–1926

There is no dearth of studies devoted to the Petrograd Museum of Artistic Culture (Muzei khudozhestvennoi kul'tury) or its more famous successor, the State Institute of Artistic Culture (Gosudarstvenny institut khudozhestvennoi kul'tury).[1] Previous works have established the basic chronology of this organization's evolution from art museum to research institute, described the various strands of Russian modernism that flourished within the walls of the building on St. Isaac's Square, and identified the individual artists who worked there. However, very little attention has been devoted to the task of situating this institutional transformation as a whole within the specific political, economic, and ideological context of NEP Russia. Nor has it ever been seen through the lens of political clientism, which, as this chapter will demonstrate, is crucial for understanding how political maneuvering on the part of two successive networks of modernist artists shaped the transformation of the Museum of Artistic Culture into the State Institute of Artistic Culture. As in Chapter Two, the figure of Kazimir Malevich, as both Soviet arts administrator and political broker, looms large in this third and final example of the "sovietization" of the Russian modernists. For it is the members of the Vitebsk/UNOVIS network that made the most radical changes in the life of an institution that was initially imagined as nothing more than the Petrograd branch of Moscow's Museum of Painterly Culture. Already under the directorship of Andrii Taran (1886–1967), the Petrograd Museum of Artistic Culture had begun to cultivate an independent identity and, more importantly, an independent operating budget, which allowed it to become a multifaceted Soviet art museum, dedicated to exhibitions and public education. In an expanded research wing, modernist works of art that had been taken out of the public domain served as research material in the various "scientific laboratories." Just a year later, the museum became an official "institute" and received a new name that explicitly elided "artistic" and "state" priorities. The very fact that the founder of Suprematism formally assumed the job of running a government-funded art organization and personally oversaw its transition from museum to state institute bespeaks the great extent to which artists themselves participated in the standardization and ultimate homogenization of Soviet visual culture.

The Origins of the Petrograd Museum of Artistic Culture

The Museum of Artistic Culture began life in 1919 as the Petrograd branch of the Moscow Museum of Painterly Culture, a Soviet institution that as we saw in Chapter One was run by modernist artists who arrogated to themselves the task of directing the activities of branch museums throughout Soviet Russia and regularly used state funds to purchase works (largely) from their fellow modernists. Despite the financial irregularities and organizational chaos that plagued the Moscow Museum Bureau, by 1920 the Petrograd Museum of Artistic Culture had received several modernist works of art—including those by Natalia Goncharova, Rodchenko, Liubov' Popova, and Udal'tsova—from the collection of paintings in Moscow.[2] More importantly, the Petrograd Museum of Artistic Culture was allowed to acquire works of art for itself, and was issued two million rubles' worth of credits to do so.[3] Although very little documentary evidence can be found relating to this early period of the museum's existence,[4] we know that by February 1921 there were 330 works of art in the museum, including paintings and drawings by Lev Bruni, Marc Chagall, Alexander Miturich, Alexandre Benois, and Mstislav Dobuzhinsky, as well those by Sergei Chekhonin (1878–1936), a member of the Collegium of the Fine Arts Department of the Petrograd Narkompros, and Natan Al'tman, the head of the Petrograd Fine Arts Department, who was entrusted by his Moscow counterpart (David Shterenberg) with the task of supervising the newly founded museum and its growing collection. Although the resulting holdings did indeed reflect the stated policy of acquiring representatives of all trends in art, the modernists were clearly favored by the Petrograd artist-administrators who implemented it and who were some of its main beneficiaries.[5] And records indicate that acquisitions would continue into 1921, despite the fact that as late as December 1920 the "museum [had not yet] managed to finish the necessary repairs" to the building, which was on a piece of prime real estate, in St. Isaac's Square.[6] Although the new museum was "projected to open on January 1," the staff of the Petrograd Museum of Artistic Culture did not actually begin admitting the general public until sometime in April 1921.[7] And when they did, Soviet museum-goers were confronted by "pictures" that were "displayed not in historical-chronological order" but rather according to "methods of artistic production," a decision that clearly reflected the ideas of the Moscow Museum of Painterly Culture's artist-curators and their well-placed friends within the Soviet state bureaucracy such as Shterenberg and Al'tman.[8]

Even the museum's transfer to the management of the Art Department of the Academic Center, the institutional precursor to the Main Scientific Administration (Glavnauka), in July 1921 could not undermine the relationships sustained by such informal ties.[9] The unplanned bureaucratic reorganization and subsequent marginalization of the Fine Arts Department apparently made Al'tman's position as head of this department (and the museum) untenable, and in September 1921 he ceded the directorship of the museum to yet another modernist artist.[10] The new director was none other than Andrii Taran, a Ukrainian-born painter whom Al'tman and Shterenberg had probably first met in Paris.[11] Taran had previously studied at the Penza Art School, where he overlapped with Vladimir Tatlin, a member of the triumvirate that made up the Museum of Artistic Culture's "Standing Committee." From the beginning, Taran's working relationship with Tatlin, Nikolai Punin, and Mikhail Matiushin (1861–1934) was so close that one Russian scholar has even argued that Al'tman's successor was only nominally the head of the Petrograd Museum of Artistic Culture, and that the driving forces behind the museum's activities in the period before Malevich's arrival were actually Punin and Tatlin.[12] Whatever the case may be, there is no doubt that in an effort to secure the support of an increasingly science-oriented bureaucratic apparatus, this small, close-knit group of modernists worked together to reorient the museum from an institution devoted to staging exhibitions to one dedicated primarily to conducting research, in effect laying the groundwork for the museum's eventual transformation into the State Institute of Artistic Culture.

We can observe this gradual metamorphosis through a series of meeting minutes and institutional reports dating from the last quarter of 1921. For example, in his very first report about the museum's activities from April to October 1921, Andrii Taran made it clear that his institution's focus was on "contemporary trends" of painting, from "impressionism to dynamic cubism." This modernist orientation was clearly reflected in the museum's organizational structure, which included departments devoted to "painterly and plastic culture, drawings and graphics, and industrial arts," such as glass-, crystal-, and porcelain-making. In a not-too-subtle call for additional space, Taran made sure to point out that the items produced by these departments could not be placed on display due to lack of sufficient accommodations. Although he claimed that museum activities over the specified period had been curtailed by the current financial situation, Taran went on to enumerate the various public debates and lectures that the museum staff had organized in the last six months, as well as all the works of art acquired or distributed to provincial museums. Having made an implicit argument about the efficiency and public-mindedness of the Petrograd Museum of Artistic Culture, Taran closed his report by asking his superiors for more funds.[13] What those funds were intended for was made apparent one month later. In November 1921, the newly formed "Museum Commission," composed of Tatlin, Punin, Vladimir Denisov (1887–1970),[14] Nikolai Lapshin (1888–1942),[15] and Taran himself, adopted a resolution to "form a scholarly institution" for artists and critics. According to the terms of this document, the museum was to be subdivided into four departments ("Collections, Exhibitions, Research, and Publications")[16] and organized along the same lines as the Marxist-oriented Academy of the History of Material Culture and the Institute of the History of Art.[17] Although Punin, the author of this resolution, benefited directly from having a departmental home in the "research" sector for art critics, he was not the only one to see the practical value of this new initiative: Malevich, upon his arrival the subsequent summer, would find the new structure conducive to the establishment of his own "laboratory" on the premises of the museum for "research work."[18]

In December 1921, Taran submitted a very optimistic "Summary of Activities Planned for 1922."[19] While confirming the museum's gradual shift toward a more systematic and objective approach to the study and display of art, this document also made it clear that the founders of the Petrograd Museum of Artistic Culture intended to stay true to the goals articulated in October 1921, albeit with a few significant additions (such as research labs). By and large, the museum was still committed to collecting and displaying its growing collection of modernist art, produced by "professional artists," as well as to introducing the Soviet public to modernism via museum tours, lectures, traveling exhibitions, and publications. However, the language that Taran used to describe these museum activities became much more inflected with materialist and "scientific" terms, evincing signs of a calculated if rather clumsy attempt to create the image of an institution in line with the most recent pronouncements on Soviet museums. This was most evident in his portrayal of the laboratories in the museum's newly formed "experimental department," which was supposed to focus on "formal construction and technique . . . aspects of technical labor and professional accomplishments," and "experiments on modes of painterly and plastic expression." Even the way the Petrograd Museum of Artistic Culture distributed works of art to other museums was supposed to proceed "according to a strict scientific plan."[20] No matter how forced the optimism or stilted the language, or rather, precisely because of it, Taran's "Summary of Activities" serves as concrete proof of the director's attempts to create an appropriately Soviet context for his museum's collection of modernist art.

At the same time, the document's totally unrealistic projections, which were invalidated only two months after being put on paper, also point to the limits of Soviet institutional self-fashioning. The optimistic plans outlined in Taran's "Summary of Activities" were derailed in early 1922, when the continuing reorganization of Narkompros and the implementation of the New Economic Policy caused wide-scale layoffs and budget cuts. In February 1922, M. P. Kristi, the director of the Petrograd office of the Main Scientific Administration, announced Narkompros's decision to consolidate the Petrograd Museum of Artistic Culture with its parent institution in Moscow, rename it the Petrograd Division of the Museum of Painterly Culture, and cut its staff almost by half (from sixteen to nine people).[21] Although the threatened consolidation never actually took place, the layoffs did, despite Kristi's best efforts to help Taran get funding for two new positions ("a curator and a guard").[22] The Main Scientific Administration's attempt to centralize and assert administrative control over the two fairly autonomous museums was a sign of things to come, for it squared well with other priorities put forward by the designers of the NEP, especially financial and ideological accountability.[23] However, of more immediate concern was the effect of the budget cuts, which made financial difficulties a harsh reality. The museum made almost no acquisitions between the end of 1921 and the first half of 1922, relying on exchanges with other museums for new exhibitions. It even started charging for services that it used to provide gratis. For example, in spring 1922, the Petrograd Museum of Artistic Culture demanded payment from the Russian Museum ("in view of NEP") for some works of art transferred to the latter.[24] Money for wages and operating costs was so consistently late that Taran could not even afford postage and had to ask the post office to extend the museum some credit.[25]

Despite what seem like insurmountable difficulties, in May 1922 the museum was able to mount one of the most ambitious art exhibitions in early Soviet history. The impetus for this exhibition came from Vladimir Tatlin, who, as we saw, was one of the leading figures in the life of the Petrograd Museum of Artistic Culture in the period preceding the arrival of Malevich. Although his studio was initially at the former Academy of Arts (recently renamed the Petrograd Higher State Artistic and Technical Studios), Tatlin was an active member of the Museum of Artistic Culture's administration, and had known many of its employees, including Punin, Nikolai Lapshin (1888–1942, graphic artist, painter), and Nikolai Tyrsa for almost ten years. Even the apartment in which he lived with his wife and young son was in the same building as the museum.[26] So when Mikhail Matiushin, Tatlin's colleague (who had been evicted from his studio at the Academy of Arts by the Petrograd Department of the Administration of Professional Education) moved his own studio over to the Museum of Artistic Culture, Tatlin followed suit.[27] Safely ensconced among a familiar network of friends and colleagues, the "flying Dutchman of modern Russian art history" seemed to have finally found a safe harbor.[28] In fact, this very sense of safety may have given him the confidence to go on the offensive. That may explain why, in early 1922, Tatlin wrote a letter to the Academic Center denouncing the work of his colleagues at the Russian Museum. In that letter, Tatlin complained that "in the Russian Museum, a significant number of the works of the so-called left artists, which have been acquired at various times over eight years, are not exhibited in the public rooms, but are kept in storage, and some of the works previously shown have been removed." However, he argued, a "comprehensive knowledge of the state of contemporary Russian art for visitors to the Russian Museum is possible only if space is given . . . equally to all tendencies worthy of it, on the basis of their . . . importance in art." Tatlin then suggested that a representative of "new tendencies," such as the author himself, should be made a permanent member of the board of the Russian Museum to prevent this type of imbalance in the future.[29]

Tatlin did not wait for the authorities to look into the exhibitions policy at the Russian Museum, however. In an effort to redress the fact that his and his colleagues' works were not on view anyplace else, Tatlin decided to use the resources of the Petrograd Museum of Artistic Culture to organize the exhibition himself. The resulting "Survey of New Trends in Art," which was staged in the galleries of the museum, was intended to showcase "all the artistic forces of Petrograd working in the areas of the new art, in painting, theater, music, sculpture, and architectural design."[30] According to the leaflet printed for the exhibition, the Soviet "masses" who attended this event would become acquainted with the over one hundred works of "new art" through "lectures, discussions, and excursions."[31] Unfortunately, the entrance fees were set prohibitively high for 1922 and only one hundred fifty people came over a six-day period.[32] Low attendance notwithstanding, the show truly was inclusive of artists of all trends, exhibiting the works of modernist artists such as Lev Bruni, as well as A. Andreev of the ProletKul't, a group that promoted artists from the proletariat, alongside those created by such famous practitioners of abstraction as Malevich, and of course, Tatlin himself.[33] While Tatlin's motives were clearly self-serving, it can nevertheless be argued that he, like the institution to which he belonged and which sponsored this exhibition, sought not only to prove his willingness to play along with official arts policy—inasmuch as it had been formulated by this time[34]—but also to demonstrate that his own work should be seen as part of the new Soviet world, rather than part of the decadent, bourgeois world that the Soviets left behind.[35]

The Vitebsk UNOVIS Network

During the fall of 1922 and spring of 1923, the museum was concerned with a variety of tasks: reinstalling the permanent collection after the exhibition "Survey of New Trends in Art," arranging lectures, and putting together a catalog of the museum's collection. Thanks to Kristi, the Petrograd branch of the Main Scientific Administration even agreed to fund this publication, as long as the text about the new art in the museum was "of a popular character."[36] But perhaps the most important development in the life of Museum of Artistic Culture was the arrival of Malevich and the Vitebsk UNOVIS network. Their arrival in Petrograd, in August 1922, coincided with the expulsion of over two hundred members of the intelligentsia from Soviet Russia: writers, professors, and scientists were imprisoned and then ordered to leave the country, having been accused of "anti-Soviet" activities. As Stuart Finkel has argued, this was part of an effort to send a strong message about the proper place for public intellectuals in a socialist society: they were to work for the people only as directed by a dictatorship of the proletariat. Any attempt to define their tasks independently of the collective dictum would be interpreted as anti-Soviet. While the expulsions were the most stunning events during the anti-intelligentsia campaigns of 1922–23, most nonparty institutions, including museums, experienced a dramatic increase in the monitoring of their activities, among many other restrictive measures.[37]

Malevich and his colleagues were keenly aware that any intellectual activity in a Soviet art institution would have to be in accordance with the demands of the directives of the Main Scientific Administration. Their experience in Vitebsk, where UNOVIS first engaged in a more-or-less successful attempt to adapt—both discursively and practically—to new Soviet realities in an effort to reshape them according to the tenets of Suprematism, prepared the new arrivals well for what they would encounter in Petrograd. As in Vitebsk, their response to increased state intervention was not heroic resistance or sullen foot-dragging, but the establishment of a "research laboratory" specifically devoted to, and run by, individuals associated with "left art." This creative solution was dictated not only by the artists' aesthetic agenda, but also by more practical considerations. Artists who were sequestered in research departments were subject to far less scrutiny than public intellectuals, since they were supposedly not in positions to exert a "bad influence upon Soviet youth."[38] During the current anti-intellectual campaigns, consequently, this was the safest place to be.

Although the idea for a research unit within the Petrograd Museum of Artistic Culture arose as early as 1921, and was supported by Pavel Filonov (1883–1941), Nikolai Lapshin, and Nikolai Punin, it is significant that this institutional reorganization did not take place until four months after Malevich appeared on the scene and that it was accompanied by a small but strategic "purge" of individuals affiliated with the previous administration.[39] In December 1922, Malevich and his supporters finally managed to establish a research laboratory on the premises of the Museum of Artistic Culture.[40] Concurrently, three staff members were laid off, thereby reducing the total number of paid artists in residence to sixteen, and increasing the relative weight of the Vitebsk network.[41] Of the previous administrative group, only Tatlin, Punin, Taran, Lapshin, and Nikolai Tyrsa remained on staff. Although Taran remained nominally in charge for another six months, he had effectively become a lame duck. Power had shifted to the new research unit, which served as the basis of a "family circle," with Malevich as patriarch. By early 1923, museum reports begin to include descriptions of the research activities being conducted by Malevich, Punin, Matiushin, and Tatlin, the future departmental heads at the State Institute of Artistic Culture (see figure 10). For example, the official report for the first half of 1923 reflects a wide range of activities for the public. The museum's modern art collection was reinstalled and 2,416 people reportedly came to see it. Additionally, museum staff hosted twenty excursions for a total of over eight hundred people. The report boasted a series of lectures read by Punin, Ermolaeva, Lapshin, Malevich, Matiushin, and Tatlin on "questions of contemporary art and artistic culture" which reportedly "incited lively discussion." Not to be outdone, Malevich gave four lectures, including "God Is Not Cast Down" and "New Proofs in Art."[42]

At the same time, Tatlin used his "laboratory" at the Museum of Artistic Culture to realize one of the most modernist of theatrical events: a staged performance of *Zangezi,* a poem by the recently deceased Futurist poet Velimir Khlebnikov (1885–1922), whose manuscripts, printed works, and drawings were exhibited at the Museum of Artistic Culture. The text of *Zangezi* was composed of trans-rational (*zaum*) language, bird sounds, as well as "astral" language, and the poem culminated in a war of the letters of the alphabet. It was performed against a backdrop of Tatlin's counter-reliefs and

Figure 10. Unknown photographer, department heads, *left to right,* Nikolai Punin, Kazimir Malevich, and Mikhail Matiushin at the State Institute of Artistic Culture, Leningrad. 1925.

architectonic drawings (see figure 11).[43] Although *Zangezi* showcased both men's inclinations toward formal and verbal experimentation, and reordering the universe according to alogical principles, in his published description of the production, Tatlin adopted a more populist rhetoric: he characterized his own role as making "Khlebnikov's creative work accessible to the masses" and justified his decision to rely on the talents of students rather than professional actors by the need to "better mobilize young people untouched by the theater, so as to reveal Khlebnikov's work as a revolutionary event."[44]

Considering the severe financial constraints within which it operated, the museum's wide-ranging activities might appear as nothing less than miraculous. It helped, however, that the new administration continued to receive the helpful advice, if not always the needed financial support, of Kristi, the museum's patron at the Petrograd branch of the Main Scientific Administration. For example, in January 1923 Lapshin, the temporary acting director of the Petrograd Museum of Artistic Culture, appealed to Kristi for a one-time expenditure of 375 rubles to install a telephone, "to establish a connection between the museum and state institutions." Kristi, who was tasked with implementing directives insisting that institutions that were still on the state budget should try to raise their own funds and be somewhat self-supporting, denied Lapshin's request. One week later, however, the assistant director of the Museum of Artistic Culture asked if the museum

Figure 11. Unknown photographer, set of *Zangezi* at the Museum of Artistic Culture, Petrograd. 1922.

could organize a free lecture series on Sundays. This time the head of the Petrograd section of the Main Scientific Administration gave his consent, but advised his correspondent that an admission fee had to be levied to "improve the economic situation of the museum."[45] But this correspondence between patron and client was not unidirectional. For example, in February 1923, Kristi himself wrote a letter to Lapshin in which he suggested that the museum begin charging admission fees (which, he immediately specified, should be waived for art school students and Red Army soldiers).[46] The museum administration eventually came around to the idea of submitting to the demands of the (managed) marketplace promoted by the designers of the NEP and, at the beginning of May 1923, the Petrograd Museum of Artistic Culture started charging a general admission fee.[47]

The museum's active program, and its avowed orientation toward the Soviet public, however, did not imply universal approval of its activities. In fact, the spring of 1923 witnessed the publication of a flurry of articles criticizing the Petrograd Museum of Artistic Culture. For example, a reporter for *Late News* (*Poslednie izvestiia*) testified that the museum collection was "utterly incomprehensible for the masses." Another correspondent falsely reported about the poor state of preservation of works in the museum. "Why do they hate this small and comparatively rarely visited museum?" asked Punin in an article published in *The Life of Art*. "Who is it bothering?" Punin, like many of his colleagues, was not a person who was content merely with asking plaintive rhetorical questions. His polemical piece was in fact a carefully argued response to another article in *The Life of Art* in which S. K. Isakov praised the work of the large main museums and called the Museum of Artistic Culture "unnecessary," probably the strongest possible censure during the NEP era.[48] In his reply to Isakov's critique, Punin argued that the Petrograd Museum of Artistic Culture was founded precisely as a rebuke to the larger museums, which were unable to realize their goals as cultural-educational institutions. He noted that the museum would only become unnecessary when large museums "completely and consciously turned away from domination of dead and false-scientific structures." After cleverly turning Isakov's critique against him, Punin then offered several justifications for the existence of the Museum of Artistic Culture. As an independent center of museum expertise, the Museum of Artistic Culture shattered the monopoly imposed by the traditional system of state museums. Only such a museum, Punin averred, could revitalize the tradition of museums in general. He admitted that the current collection, which consisted only of new art, was less popular with museumgoers than that of older, more traditional museums. But, as Soviet citizens knew full well, the new and revolutionary was always difficult at first. Unlike the well-known, staid, and conservative venues defended by Isakov, the Museum of Artistic Culture welcomed the new art. After all, Punin concluded, it had to go somewhere.[49] From this perspective, the Museum of Artistic Culture was a useful alternative, which was intended not to completely replace traditional museums, but to temporarily fulfill a very specific purpose: that of accommodating and preserving the new, revolutionary art created by Punin's modernist colleagues.

From Museum of Artistic Culture to State Institute of Artistic Culture

In June 1923, Andrii Taran officially resigned his post as director of the Petrograd Museum of Artistic Culture and accepted an invitation from the Ukrainian Academy of Painting to head up the studio of monumental painting in Kiev.[50] His departure marked the end of an era for the modernists in the Museum of Artistic Culture. As we saw, the work carried out during Taran's tenure represented a search for compromise: the collection of chiefly modernist art was on exhibit but the museum staff attempted to create an appropriately egalitarian yet scholarly context for it by arranging excursions and public lectures by the artists themselves. Moving away from the notion of museum as exhibition space, the Taran administration also oversaw the creation of a "scientific commission" and approved Malevich's request to organize a research laboratory on its premises, in effect sowing the seeds for the State Institute of Artistic Culture. It was under Malevich's stewardship, however, that the staff of the Petrograd Museum of Artistic Culture made a conscious commitment to transform their organization into a purely research-oriented facility. As the following analysis will demonstrate, they did so not only to secure funding and support for their increasingly beleaguered organization, or to provide space for artists to work on experimental and socially transformative art, but also to meet party and state mandates for a systematic artistic practice.

Although Malevich and his circle had assumed control of the Museum of Artistic Culture earlier in the year, formal control still resided in the Museum Commission, which as late as August 1923 was still composed of Punin, Tatlin, and Lapshin. The minutes from a July 1923 meeting of the Museum Commission demonstrate the pressure that the members of this body faced from the Malevich network, which was arguing in favor of continuing and expanding earlier efforts to reorient the museum toward research. During the course of the July meeting, Lapshin, who had taken over the duties of temporary director of the Museum of Artistic Culture after Taran's departure, raised the issue of the future work of the museum. To this Punin replied that the museum should focus on "ideologically strengthening the position of new art," or in other words, attempting to situate modern art in an appropriately Soviet context. Tatlin, who seems to have been aware that funding would be forthcoming for "laboratory" work, then expressed his concern over the "weak connection of the museum with laboratory research work." He argued that it was necessary to strengthen this connection, not only to avoid the separation of the labs from the museum but also to develop the labs as "uniquely necessary for the realization of the museum's material base."[51] By August, however, the members of the Museum Commission had come to an understanding with Malevich and formally nominated him to the post of director, thereby ceding control of the museum's governing body to the leader of the Vitebsk network. Kristi approved of the nomination and Malevich became the official director in early August 1923.[52]

Malevich's first task upon becoming the director of the Museum of Artistic Culture was the organization of four new research laboratories within the museum. The staffing of the new organizational units reflected his earlier deal with Museum Commission members, who received positions in the new administration: Punin became chair of the Department of General Ideology, Tatlin—the Department of Material Culture, and Matiushin (who had been part of the triumvirate that constituted Taran's Standing Committee)—the Department of Organic Culture. The new director of the Museum of Artistic Culture, meanwhile, arrogated to himself the chairmanship of the Formal-Theoretical Department.[53] Malevich next tried to find an appropriate name for this new research structure: in September 1923 he requisitioned thirty easels from the Academy of Arts for the "Institute of Artistic Knowledge."[54] One month later, he called the organization the "Institute of Higher Artistic Knowledge."[55] Two months after that, the Museum of Artistic Culture's newly revised charter referred to the "Research Institute of Artistic Labor," a designation that, as we can see, was the product of Malevich's deliberate efforts to christen his new institution with a lofty yet proletarian-sounding name.[56] The "Research Institute of Artistic Labor's" new charter, which was submitted to the Main Scientific Administration in December 1923, marked an important moment of transition in yet another sense: it signaled the museum's new identity as a research institution, while relegating the educational and museological functions to the back burner. This shift was reflected not only in its new name, but also by the fact that museum activities were not described until the very last section of the document. The museum and its collection were thus presented as an appendage, a small department within a well-organized scholarly research institution devoted to formulating a "scientifically based method of research about art, its role, and the meaning of art in life."[57]

In this, as in so many other respects, the text of the Museum of Artistic Culture's 1923 charter is strikingly similar to that of the State Academy of Artistic Research (GAKhN). Founded in 1921 in Moscow as an institute for the study and research about art within the Marxist-Leninist framework, the Academy of Artistic Research was the ideal revolutionary institution. So much so that in 1922, the commissar of enlightenment himself described it as "one of the most important Academic-artistic institutions of the republic."[58] Lunacharsky's patronage may explain why such diverse artists as Kandinsky and Konstanin Yuon were counted among its members. Between 1923 and 1925, Malevich not only was a member, but also regularly gave speeches and participated in meetings.[59] He undoubtedly had access to the academy's charters and plans, which described that institution's commitment to the "the creation of a science about painting, not only for its own sake, but for practical use."[60] The Academy of Artistic Research's purpose was further described in 1923 as "comprehensive scientific research" related to questions of art . . . and artistic culture . . . and unifying the scientific activity of artistic institutions in the republic." In describing his own fiefdom, now named the "Scientific-Research Institute of Artistic Labor," Malevich articulated similarly objective goals:

> The Scientific-Research Institute of Artistic Labor, like other scientific-research institutions, carries out work in the area of art. The Institute's tasks are a) carrying out research . . . in the area of contemporary art . . . beginning with analysis of the ideology and history of art; b) develop a scientifically based method of research on art, its role, and the meaning of art in life; c) application of art methods; and d) scientific criticism of art.[61]

Even closer are Yuon's July 1923 description of his subdepartment of painting within the academy and Malevich's description of the Formal-Theoretical Department. Yuon describes the work of his department as carrying out analytical approaches of all manifestations of painting, in its technical and historical aspects: "The final goal of our work is the creation of a science about painting." Finally Yuon's plan specified five elements of paintings which, through analysis, would reveal an objective science of art: form, color, light, material, and space. The plan also specified that tables and diagrams should be made to reveal the results of this research.[62]

Malevich's plan for his Formal-Theoretical Department resembles, in spirit at the very least, Yuon's description for the analogous department: the department's task is described as "revealing the systems . . . of art, the environment creating these manifestations, and the process of historical development." Malevich described the aspects of art as "form, structure, texture, construction and colors." His methodological approach? "Painting as science."[63] By adopting a materialist approach to studying and codifying art, both artists incorporated a strong Marxist element in the work of their departments.[64] And in a December 1923 letter to the Main Scientific Administration, in which Malevich attempted to validate his own institute's work and justify commensurate funding and ideological support, the new director even directly compared his institute with the Academy of Artistic Research.[65] This may seem surprising, given that, as Nicoletta Misler states, the Academy of Artistic Research was a "venerable, dignified institution that had little to do with the Avant Garde," and at best had an ambivalent attitude toward it.[66] And yet it was exactly this status that Malevich sought for his "Research Institute of Artistic Labor," albeit on a much smaller scale.

His reasons for doing so are not hard to fathom. By reducing the role of the museum collection within the self-described research institute, and by mimicking the more successful Academy of Artistic Research, Malevich clearly sought to avoid the fate of the Moscow Museum of Painterly Culture, which was transferred to the jurisdiction of the Main Museum Administration in May 1923. As we saw in Chapter One, after the transfer of the paintings, the Moscow museum spent much of its time closed, was annexed by the Tretyakov Gallery in 1924, and lost its own budget and its entire art collection by 1925. By 1924, in contrast, Malevich had written a new charter for the—now Leningrad—Museum of Artistic Culture, one that transformed it into a research institute, and had already submitted it to the Main Scientific Administration. There was no guarantee that Malevich's request would be granted, of course, and political developments did not appear especially favorable. That year had witnessed a dramatic increase in Communist Party interventions in the artistic arena. Within two months of Lenin's death in early 1924, the Communist Party began replacing nonparty "specialists" in the Soviet arts apparatus with party members, to solidify its control of the cultural sphere. Within the Communist Party itself there was a push for a unified arts policy, and party officials openly supported proletarian writers' groups in their bid for literary hegemony and the Association of Artists of Revolutionary Russia as the new standard for painting.[67] These developments were accompanied by a sharp increase in attacks against "left art." A widely read, programmatic article in *Sovetskoe iskusstvo* (*Soviet Art*) "About a Single Arts Policy," for example, condemned "all experiments: Futurism, Suprematism, Constructivism" as trash and lamented the fact that new (Communist) artistic principles had not been created.[68]

As non-Communists within the Art Department of the Main Scientific Administration began to be replaced by party members, research institutions were required to prove that they were not solely devoted to the study of the theory and history of art, but also that their activity satisfied the demands of the working masses.[69] This increased stress on assessment and accountability, as well as uncertainty about the outcome of his request for official recognition, may explain why in 1924 the activities of the "Research Institute of Artistic Labor" closely reflected the imperatives laid out by Glavnauka's Art Department, as well as why they were couched in the politically correct fashion. Malevich, who had been known to refer to himself as a "doctor," adopted the clinical tone of a lab worker, and the other department chairs followed suit.[70] For example, Malevich wrote that his Formal-Theoretical Department planned to "establish an analytical approach to painting" out of which would develop a new objective approach to teaching art.[71] Punin followed suit, describing the work of his department as the "creation of scientific criticism, based on the solid base of a scientific approach to art."[72]

Responding to the Main Scientific Administration's call for closer connections between research activities and the Soviet public, Tatlin, the chair of the Material Culture Department, titled his May 1924 lecture "Material Culture and Its Role in Production and Everyday Life in the USSR." To drum up an appropriately proletarian audience, he then wrote a letter to Grigory Yatmanov, the deputy director of the Petrograd Art Department and former colleague of Tatlin within the Narkompros Department of Fine Arts, in which he issued an exclusive invitation to "Communists, union leaders, [and] members of factory administrations" and explained that his lecture would focus on how artist-constructors would be connected with factories and the general organization of the new life. He signed the letter "With comradely greetings" (*s tovarishchskim privetom*).[73]

It must have been a huge relief when, in late September 1924, Malevich finally received word that the Main Scientific Administration had formally recognized the subordination of the museum to the research institute. Although the name change from Museum of Artistic Culture to the State Institute of Artistic Culture did not take effect until October 1924, Malevich and his colleagues had just cause to celebrate.[74] Despite an increasingly hostile political environment, they succeeded in preventing the closure of their "leftist" art organization. Better yet, they managed to persuade the authorities to recognize it as part of the growing network of state-sponsored research institutes. Official recognition, in turn, affected the balance of power within the State Institute of Artistic Culture itself. Malevich's success reaffirmed his charismatic status and served to consolidate his special position of authority among Leningrad's modernists in general, and the Vitebsk network in particular. The director of the State Institute of Artistic Culture was now the undisputed master and the newly recognized institute was his personal domain: its status and power were inseparable from the man in charge. Malevich acted as the paterfamilias for a circle of loyal clients, who worked together to deflect criticism and to keep challenges at bay by presenting a united front to government officials. If even one person decided to flaunt the practices or question the values of this family circle, he or she could put the entire enterprise in jeopardy. At the State Institute of Artistic Culture, this person was Tatlin.

Tatlin and Malevich had a long and complicated history. Their professional rivalry and personal animosity, however, did not come to a head until immediately after Malevich became the undisputed leader of the State Institute of Artistic Culture, that is, after he had abandoned the practice of consulting with the members of the former Museum Commission. Tatlin, who had held an important executive role at the Museum of Artistic Culture before Malevich's arrival in Petrograd, chafed under the latter's dictatorial leadership style and was not afraid to demonstrate his disaffection from the clique that held the reins of power.[75] Publicly, Malevich maintained a respectful distance and refused to comment on the topic. In private correspondence, however, Malevich dismissed his obstreperous but talented colleague as an "idiot."[76] The break between the State Institute of Artistic Culture's director and the chair of the Material Culture Department went public at the worst possible time. In October 1924, during an inspection of the institute, representatives of the Main Scientific Administration had censured Tatlin for "isolating himself" from the rest of the collective.[77] The next month, Tatlin refused to appear at an important meeting, during which all department heads were scheduled to present their work to inspectors from the Main Scientific Administration. This act of flagrant insubordination was the last straw. Rather than risk the institution's censure, and possible closure, Malevich immediately distanced himself from Tatlin, so that he and only he would take the fall. However, his stratagem did not work out as planned. F. K. Lekht (1887–1961), the head of the Art Department within the Main Scientific Administration in Leningrad and the official in charge of the inspection of the State Institute of Artistic Culture, had agreed to fire Tatlin on the spot. However, in an effort to improve the State Institute of Artistic Culture's commitment to Communist Party values (*partiinost'*), and perhaps to break up the Malevich family circle, he decided to replace the modernist who chaired the Department of Material Culture with Tikhon Chernyshev (1882–1942), a member of the Association of Artists of Revolutionary Russia, the art organization of which Lekht himself was one of the founding fathers.

Tatlin, however, refused to budge.[78] And the longer he stayed on the premises of the institute, the more worried Malevich became. In a letter to Punin, written in the spring of 1925, Malevich expressed concern that Tatlin and his former student Pavel Mansurov (1896–1983), would sabotage the next inspection by not adhering to the "unified" line of the Institute of Artistic Culture's policies.[79] In other words, if they refused to play along, these prodigal sons would jeopardize the entire family circle of which he was the paterfamilias. Malevich had legitimate reasons for concern: the Main Scientific Administration inspectors had already branded Tatlin as a "poorly educated . . . psychologically abnormal . . . paranoiac," who was disruptive of "the normal life of the institute."[80] And Mansurov, in his capacity as head of the Experimental Department at the Institute of Artistic Culture, had been completely uncooperative during a December 1924 inspection, not allowing the inspectors to see the current work of the department and prompting them to conclude that the department was "unsuccessful."[81] When, in 1926, Mansurov issued his "manifesto" at a State Institute of Artistic Culture exhibition in which he decried "the ideas of administrators . . . and politicians" that have no relevance for contemporary artists, Malevich sought to distance himself and his institute from the views of the chair of the Experimental Department by describing the claims made in Mansurov's polemical publication as "provocations."[82] The institute's director simply could not appear to support Mansurov's diatribe against state intervention in the arts, no matter how much he agreed with the latter's call for a turn away from Cubo-Futurism and toward utilitarianism and technology.

The End of the State Institute of Artistic Culture

When Tatlin finally decamped to Kiev, in the spring of 1925, the State Institute of Artistic Culture's administration was finally able to turn its attention away from personnel problems and to focus on its regular activities. Even a brief analysis of the Institute of Artistic Culture's budget proposal from spring 1925 demonstrates that its authors sought to align their priorities with the mission statement that the Commissariat of Enlightenment had drawn up for all Soviet research institutes. Narkompros's mission statement, which was published in January 1925, tasked Soviet institutes with first studying questions from a scientific point of view and then with popularizing that scientific knowledge.[83] In an effort to address the first point, and to underline the scientific, or at least systematic, nature of their work, Malevich, Punin, and Matiushin decided to supplement the narrative descriptions of the activities of their respective departments with these charts.

This table depicts Malevich's Formal-Theoretical Department at a glance (see table 2 and figure 12). It was intended to show that this particular department of the State Institute of Artistic Culture was responsible for analyzing both specific works of art and the sociological circumstances under which they arose, along with the historical development of artistic systems in general. Analogous tables demonstrated that Matiushin's Department of Organic Culture focused on audience perception, while the aim of Punin's General Ideology Department was to establish an exact and objective art criticism (see tables 3 and 4).[84] To address the second point in Narkompros's mission statement for research institutes, the State Institute of Artistic Culture department heads vowed not only to expand their organization's cultural and educational activities, such as conducting excursions in the museum, but also to encourage their researchers to form collaborative cooperatives and pursue collective rather than individual research projects.[85] Their efforts were clearly not in vain, because Malevich received formal authorization to pursue the activities described in the Institute of Artistic

Table 2. Formal-Theoretical Department (Artistic Culture)

Research of Systems in Art: Impressionism, Cezannism, Cubism, Futurism, Suprematism		**Theoretical Office**	**Research of the Means of Artistic Development**	
Laboratory A	Laboratory B	Basic Principles of Painterly Systems	Movement of Color in Centers of Culture	Changes in Form in Centers of Culture
Light	Line	Methods of Studied Systems		
Color	Volume	Organization of Systems		
Painting	Composition	Founders and Followers		
Tone	Construction	Connection with Production		
Contemporary Art			Contemporary Relations	
		Art as Science		

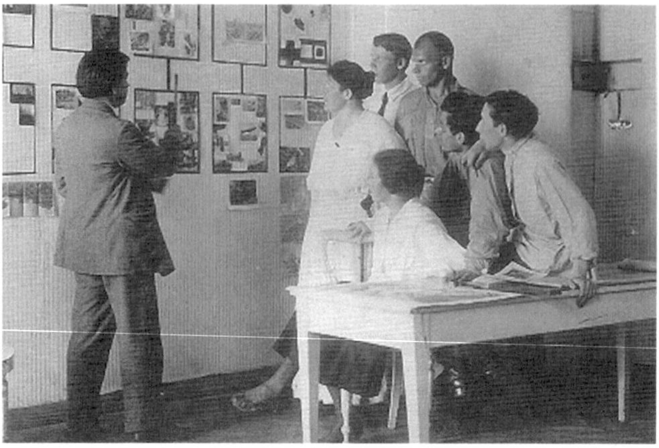

Figure 12. Unknown photographer, Kazimir Malevich and colleagues in the Formal-Theoretical Department at the State Institute of Artistic Culture (GINKhUK). About 1925.

Culture's budget proposal. Although the institute was allocated only about half of the amount of money it had requested for the 1925–26 academic year, Malevich—facing down the threat of relocation—did successfully petition to remain in the current accommodations on St. Isaacs Square, in the very center of Leningrad.[86]

The Main Scientific Administration's Art Department, the agency that approved the State Institute of Artistic Culture's budget proposal for spring 1925, spelled out its priorities and goals for fall 1925 at the Main Scientific Administration's exhibition, which was timed to coincide with the eighth anniversary of the October Revolution. The Moscow exhibition showcased the work of all ninety institutions supervised by the Main Scientific Administration, including the Institute of Artistic Culture. "Production" and "pedagogy" were the buzzwords of the day. A brochure printed for this special event listed the Art Department's goals in the following order of priority: to regulate contemporary art, establish connections with production to meet the demands of the worker-peasant state, encourage "sociological" research methods, increase the production bias in art institutions, and finally, devote more efforts to the study of peasant art.[87] Judging by the official description of its activities for 1925–26, the Institute of Artistic Culture followed its parent institution's policies very closely. Not coincidently, the work of Malevich's own department was divided into two categories: Production and Pedagogy. In the report for 1925–26, Malevich first described

Table 3. Department of Organic Culture

<table>
<tr><th colspan="12">Department of Organic Culture</th></tr>
<tr><td colspan="6">Research on Spatial Perception on Models in Laboratory and in Nature</td><td colspan="6">Research on Spatial Forms in Painting, Sculpture, Architecture, Music, Verbal Arts</td></tr>
<tr><td colspan="2">Laboratory of Vision</td><td colspan="2">Laboratory of Hearing</td><td colspan="2">Laboratory of Touch</td><td colspan="2">Office of Color-Forms</td><td colspan="2">Office of Audio-Rhythm</td><td colspan="2">Office of Surface Structure</td></tr>
<tr><td>Retinal</td><td>Vision centers</td><td>Peripheral hearing</td><td>Internal hearing</td><td>Touch</td><td>Internal senses</td><td>Structure of forms</td><td>Volume of forms</td><td>Structure of forms</td><td>Volume of forms</td><td>Structure of forms</td><td>Volume of forms</td></tr>
<tr><td colspan="2">Visual perception of any kind of vibration</td><td colspan="2">Aural perception of any kind of vibration</td><td colspan="2">Sensual perception of any kind of vibration</td><td colspan="2">Painterly expression of any kind of vibration</td><td colspan="2">Musical expression of any kind of vibration</td><td colspan="2">Sculptural expression of any kind of vibration</td></tr>
<tr><td colspan="6">Study of the Confluence of Perception</td><td colspan="6">Laws of the Confluence of Perception</td></tr>
<tr><td colspan="12">New Spatial Consciousness</td></tr>
</table>

Table 4. Department of General Ideology

Department of General Ideology				
Analytic method		Synthetic method		**General philosophy of art**
Perception of methods	Creation of form	Quality of materials	Quality of space	
Awareness of culture	System			
Painting	Artists	Material culture	Organic individual	
General theory of art				

his department's work on textiles and constructions and then outlined a pedagogical method based on his "theory of the additional element": Malevich's attempt to establish a "scientifically precise" and sociologically based explanation of every painting style.[88] Other department chairs followed the director's lead: to meet demands for production, for example, the Department of Organic Culture designed posters and kiosks, as well as popularized artistic knowledge.[89] In this connection, Malevich noted that the State Institute of Artistic Culture had installed an exhibition on "the nature of artistic culture and its connections with sociological, physiological, and psychological manifestations."[90] It is unclear exactly what was on view, but it may very well have been the charts that explicated his theory of the additional element. To further raise the pedagogical profile of the institute as a whole, Malevich asked the Main Administration of Political Education to register the State Institute of Artistic Culture as open for business and taking bookings for excursions. Finally, in January 1926, the State Institute of Artistic Culture researchers gave lectures at a conference on the study of peasant art, thereby fulfilling the last item on the Main Scientific Administration's list of priorities.[91]

And for once the bosses at the Main Scientific Administration seemed pleased. In a move that officially recognized the administrative abilities of the Institute of Artistic Culture's activist leader, Malevich was appointed as director of the foundering Decorative Arts Institute.[92] In addition to his regular responsibilities, he was charged with planning the Decorative Arts Institute's activities for 1925–26 and with coordinating the "work of the [institute] with the scientific-research activities" of the Institute of Artistic Culture.[93] Malevich's promotion, however, appears to have come with strings attached. Furthermore, his attempts to cover all fronts seem to have made him vulnerable on each. This may explain why during the spring and summer of 1926, the Decorative Arts Institute's art collection was transferred to the large State Museums in Leningrad and Moscow, despite objections that the Institute of Artistic Culture could not fulfill its educational function without the institute's historic holdings, which traced their roots back to the collecting activity of the Petrograd Museum of Artistic Culture.[94] Despite this setback, Malevich's home institution appeared to be functioning smoothly when the art critic Grigorii Ginger (1897–1994), aka "Grey Greg" (Grigorii Seryi), published his now infamous article "A State-Sponsored Monastery" in *Leningrad Pravda* (*Leningradskaia Pravda*) on June 10, 1926. Ginger used his review of the State Institute of Artistic Culture's year-end exhibition as a platform from which to launch an attack against Malevich and his modernist colleagues. Ginger deliberately employed the antireligious rhetoric of such atheistic organizations as the League of Militant Godless to denounce the staff of "holy crackpots" sequestered in the "State-Sponsored Monastery" on St. Isaac's Square. Relying on his readers' knowledge of the behavior of stereotypical Orthodox monks, Ginger pointedly accused the Institute of Artistic Culture's modernists of reckless extravagance and artistic "debauchery." What was worse, in Ginger's opinion, was that the modernists were wasting the government's money at a time "when hundreds of really talented artists [were] going hungry." Having painted a verbal picture of corruption straight out of *Atheist at the Workbench* (*Bezbozhnik u Stanka*),[95] Ginger concluded his art review by publicly accusing the Institute of Artistic Culture's modernists of "counterrevolutionary" activity.[96] The inflammatory rhetoric of "Grey Greg" was clearly intended to rile up the readers of this popular, mass-circulation daily and to prod the Main Scientific Administration and Communist Party members into action. This tactic, which had been employed in previous cases of specialist-baiting, clearly worked. As Charlotte Douglas has pointed out, an official inquiry into the goings-on at the State Institute of Artistic Culture was initiated immediately after the appearance of Ginger's review.[97]

In response to this public denunciation, the members of the State Institute of Artistic Culture's administrative team quickly sprang into action. Writing in his official capacity as director of the Scholarly Department of General Methodology (the new name for the General Ideology Department) of the State Institute of Artistic Culture, Punin fired off a letter to the Main Scientific Administration in which he offered a defense of this model Soviet research institute. Punin pointed out that the Institute of Artistic Culture had received consistent support from the Main Scientific Administration itself and that Malevich's art had recently been purchased by the state.[98] In another example of trying to maintain the circle by distancing the Institute of Artistic Culture from a less reliable member, Punin explained that Mansurov (who had drawn Ginger's special ire), had been given space in the end-of-the-year exhibition despite the fact that "his ideas do not reveal sufficient scientific objectivity."[99] However, the tactic of shifting the blame onto scapegoats did not work and the inquiry continued apace.

During the next six-month period, however, the Institute of Artistic Culture continued to operate, submit new plans, and even hire new staff members. In all, four previously unpaid researchers were put on the payroll and Boris Ender (1893–1960), a modernist painter who studied under Matiushin, was promoted to head of the new Department of Physiology.[100] In fact, despite the ongoing investigation, life seemed to go on more or less as usual. This, in turn, suggests that the closure of the Institute of Artistic Culture was not the direct or inevitable result of the inquiry.

That the closure was not imminent is further evidenced by the fact that Malevich went to Moscow later that month to negotiate the institute's budget for the 1926–27 year and to discuss the transfer of the Decorative Arts Institute to the management of the State Institute of Artistic Culture.[101] Invoking the notion of self-financing, which was the party line during the NEP, Malevich argued that the Decorative Arts Institute was "directly connected" with the industrial arts and that its transfer would allow the Institute of Artistic Culture to become financially independent from Narkompros.[102] The association with industrial arts studios and the resulting financial independence would have placed the Institute of Artistic Culture on more stable ideological ground and correspondingly guaranteed its fiscal survival, at least for a few more years. Carrying off such a coup would have required Malevich to pull some major strings, and the trip may also have included visits to his Moscow-based patrons and brokers, which were obviously not recorded in the archival documentation. However, there is evidence to show that Malevich did consult with his high-placed patron in Leningrad. Malevich's personal correspondence reveals that he met with Kristi soon after the appearance of "A State-Sponsored Monastery," and that the head of the Leningrad Department of the Main Scientific Administration reiterated his support both for the Institute of Artistic Culture and for Malevich personally, counseling him just to ignore Ginger's review.[103] It is unclear what, if any, concrete steps Kristi made on Malevich's behalf, but the fact that the Main Scientific Administration eventually did adopt Malevich's idea to merge the Institute of Artistic Culture and the Decorative Arts Institute suggests that even at this late date, Malevich's efforts on behalf of his institute were not without success.

Another piece of evidence comes from a contemporary letter, which was written by Vera Ermolaeva on July 17, 1926, that is, over a month after the publication of Ginger's review in *Leningrad Pravda:*

> Leningrad is the last citadel of new art in Russia. Everywhere, on all fronts, is the AKhRR [Association of Artists of Revolutionary Russia]. AKhRR occupies all the positions. AKhRR is the official art. AKhRR is in the Leningrad Academies and technicums . . . They have exhibitions all year round. In all this . . . Malevich with his steel will-like energy has managed to create this Institute of Artistic Culture in Leningrad, to maintain a building with exhibition space, and 16,000 rubles per year to give a small group the possibility to work.[104]

While pointing out the oppressive ideological climate, Ermolaeva's letter does not reveal concern about imminent closure. In fact, she makes a point of praising Malevich precisely for keeping the institute open and herself and her modernist colleagues employed. If anything, the comments of this longtime member of the UNOVIS group exude confidence in Malevich's indomitable "steel will" (*zheleznaia energiia*) and his ability to weather the gathering ideological storms. Despite Ermolaeva's optimism, however, it is clear that Malevich himself was concerned about the future of the State Institute of Artistic Culture. In fact, that very same month, in a private letter to Punin, Malevich went so far as to suggest the possibility of resigning from his post as director and being replaced by someone who was able to carry on the work of the institute.[105]

Although I have not been able to locate the Institute of Artistic Culture's budget plan for the 1926–27 fiscal year, Punin's "Five-Year Plan" for his Department of Methodology, drawn up in September or October 1926, has two points of interest for students of Soviet self-fashioning.[106] The first is Punin's obvious co-optation of the title for the Soviet state's massive industrialization campaign, plans for which were widely discussed during the mid-1920s, even though it was not adopted until 1928.[107] Second, Punin's plan, while far from ambitious or original, details how, year by year, one systematic step at a time, several methodological models for the study of contemporary art would be developed; in other words, how the study of contemporary art would be systematized according to a materialist taxonomic system. Most poignant, however, is Punin's belief, or at least hope, that the State Institute of Artistic Culture would operate for another five years.

While there are only a few sources to document the State Institute of Artistic Culture's activities during fall 1926, the available evidence suggests that matters were on hold until the merger with the Decorative Arts Institute was finally approved by the Main Scientific Administration.[108] However, neither the State Institute of Artistic Culture nor Malevich would be able to reap the benefits.

In a move designed to break up the family circle, Malevich was informed by the Main Scientific Administration that as of November 15, 1926, he was "freed from his duties as director of Institute of Artistic Culture" and that the institute's temporary director would be S. K. Isakov, an academic realist sculptor who had taught at the Higher Artistic-Technical Studios (VKhUTEMAS) and, ironically, the author of the *Life of Art* article that called the Museum of Artistic Culture "unnecessary." Punin, Isakov's close friend since 1915, was named deputy director and Malevich was permitted to remain on the administrative board. However, the administration was now charged with "carrying out reforms of the institute" and making arrangements that would allow its staff to fulfill "practical tasks of contemporary industrial arts"—that is, with undoing many of the procedures and policies introduced by Malevich. This reorganized institute was to be divided into two departments: Research-Theoretical and Experimental Production. Fyodr N. Petrov (1876–1973), the new director of the Main Scientific Administration, also specified that an expert in physics should be hired as soon as possible and that the State Institute of Artistic Culture should organize an exhibition for spring 1927 devoted to objects of everyday life.[109] This planned institution was never realized, however, for less than two weeks later, on December 4, 1926, the State Institute of Artistic Culture and the Decorative Arts Institute merged with the State Institute of the History of Art (GIII), and the State Institute of Artistic Culture was renamed the Committee for the Experimental Study of Artistic Culture.[110] This reorganization effectively ended the independent existence of Malevich's institute.

Although the State Institute of Artistic Culture was closed, its basic structure—perhaps due to institutional inertia—was preserved within the State Institute of the History of Art. In 1928–29, Malevich headed up a Laboratory of Painterly Culture, and Ermolaeva and Lev Yudin continued to work there with him. Matiushin and his students Maria and Boris Ender remained in the Laboratory of Organic Culture, and Suetin headed the Laboratory of Industrial Arts.[111] The merger was therefore a mixed blessing for the State Institute of Artistic Culture. Although the institute lost its autonomy, many of the modernists who staffed it not only retained research posts at the Institute of the History of Art, but also for almost three years continued working on their modernist art projects. Malevich's family circle had simply transferred to a new institutional context. The resiliency of the Malevich network was, at least in part, the result of Malevich's efforts to carve out a place in which he and his colleagues could continue to carry on experimental artistic and conceptual work during one of the most turbulent decades in Russian intellectual and cultural history. He did it by skillfully negotiating the constantly shifting landscape of political imperatives and cultural policies, shrewdly shaping his public identity, as well as that of his institute, according to the rules of Bolshevik society as it evolved over the first twelve years of Soviet rule. Such efforts at personal and institutional self-fashioning served as a key strategy for modernism's success in the Soviet political context.

Epilogue

In May 1929, upon learning that his administrative position at the State Institute of the History of Art was in serious jeopardy, Kazimir Malevich sent an urgent letter of appeal to Alexei Svidersky (1878–1933), a career party and state official who was the new director of the Main Arts Administration (Glaviskusstvo).[1] In this extended epistle, Malevich stressed the importance of the work that he and his modernist colleagues (Nikolai Suetin, Vera Ermolaeva, and Boris Ender) were carrying out at the Institute of the History of Art—work that he insisted had a "profound connection" with the demands for the "new life"—and begged his powerful addressee to intervene on their behalf.[2] As one would expect from the undisputed leader of an art group whose institutional history was inseparable from his own biography, Malevich's personal plea for support on behalf of the remnants of the core of the State Institute of Artistic Culture "family circle" took the form of an epistolary apologia pro vita sua. In an effort to legitimize his career as a Soviet modernist artist, Malevich emphasized all the ways that the Bolshevik state and its officials had supported his professional activities. He began by listing the prestigious posts that he had held since the October Revolution: head of the Art Department in the Moscow Soviet, head of the Art Department within Narkompros, and professor at VKhUTEMAS. He then claimed that as early as 1919, the assistant head of Narkompros, Mikhail Pokrovsky himself, had sent him to Vitebsk to organize "industrial art studios" (in fact, as we saw in Chapter Two, Malevich himself chose to go to the provinces during the height of the Civil War). Similarly, Malevich insisted that his government-funded "Research Institute of Artistic Culture" (one of the many names for the Petrograd Museum of Artistic Culture discussed in Chapter Three) had been instrumental in creating "new forms" for the Soviet way of life: he described, at great length, the adaptation of his Suprematist forms for porcelain designs, stating that this was one area in which he successfully employed "what is considered abstract nonobjectivity" to generate income for the state. Malevich insisted that the State Institute of Artistic Culture had received "positive reviews" from the Main Scientific Administration precisely because of its focus on production. And he averred: "At the State Institute of Artistic Culture we had one task and goal—finding new forms for architecture, textiles, shoes, furniture, and graphics." Malevich even went so far as to assert that the work of the modernists at the State Institute of Artistic Culture did not stand in opposition to that of the Association of Artists of Revolutionary Russia—the group whose platform of adhering to the reality of the working men and women of Soviet Russia served as a precursor to the doctrine of Socialist Realism—and, therefore, that he and his colleagues should by no means be considered hostile to it.[3] This appeal seemed to have worked, albeit temporarily: Malevich and his colleagues remained in their positions for another eight months, until they were expelled in early 1930, as part of a round of closures of state-operated art institutions.[4]

Malevich's letter to Svidersky is more than an illustration of the importance of personal contacts within the Soviet arts administration, a point that has been one of the main arguments of this study about the fate of the "avant-garde" under conditions of state patronage. It also testifies to the fluency in the language of Soviet officialdom that Russian modernists had acquired over the decade-and-a-half period of their employment as teachers, curators, and researchers in state-funded art institutions, such as the ones analyzed in this book. For in this letter, Malevich recounted his personal and professional history in such a way as to create an ideal portrait of the modernist painter as a Soviet arts administrator: a member of the creative, prerevolutionary intelligentsia, who despite his nonparty status, nevertheless was allied with the goals of the first socialist state in the world. Although this verbal self-portrait did indeed bear a likeness to Malevich's personal identity as it evolved since 1917, the artist's capsule autobiography, like his artwork, was more abstract than figural. That is to say, it included a lot of improvisation and personal mythmaking, or what this book has called Soviet self-fashioning.

In point of fact this epistolary example of Soviet self-fashioning had a visual analog: Malevich's solo exhibition at the State Tretyakov Gallery, which opened in 1929. How, one may ask, did an artist who was about to be fired from his post at the State Institute of the History of Art manage to get a solo exhibition at the central art museum of the Soviet Union? And how was it possible that a Suprematist exhibit could appear at the very of start of Stalin's "cultural revolution"?[5] Part of the answer to these questions lies in Malevich's choice of paintings for the exhibition. Like the biographical details in the letter to the Main Arts Administration, the modernist canvases that Malevich decided to put on public display constructed a very selective narrative of his artistic career. For example, only five paintings (including *Black Square, Black Cross,* and *Black Circle*) were Suprematist canvases, and all of these were created during the Soviet rather than the late imperial era. The rest of the paintings in the one-man exhibition were figural. Chief among these was Malevich's controversial canvases that constitute the "Peasant Cycle," most of which were substantially backdated by as many as twenty years.[6] In so doing, Malevich was creating what Charlotte Douglas has called a "new chronology,"[7] and what I would describe as an excellent example of Soviet self-fashioning: Malevich as chronicler of agrarian life, unchanged and eternal. For example, his *Landscape with Five Houses* as well as his *Female Portrait,* both of which were painted in 1928–29, were backdated to 1915, when Malevich was entirely engaged with developing Suprematist painting and theory which shunned any type of naturalistic representation (see figures 13 and 14). Furthermore, the "Peasant Cycle" paintings constitute outstanding examples of how Malevich transformed modern art into Soviet art: the paintings are certainly topical, relating to the issues of the day (namely the collectivization and rapid industrialization campaigns initiated by the first Five-Year Plan); and yet their references to the metaphysics of Giorgio de Chirico, their promise of transcendence, and their geometric, abstracted visual language made them unequivocally modern.[8]

However, as Irina Vakar has demonstrated, Malevich would not have been given the opportunity to display these modernist paintings at all if not for the support of allies and personal friends within the Tretyakov—with Kristi as director—and Main Arts Administration officials, who created the atmosphere and laid the groundwork that made this exhibition possible.[9] This observation brings us back to the importance of state patronage, political clientage, and personal networking in the rise and decline of Russian modernism. As we saw in Chapters One and Two, Russian modernists were invited to take up key positions within the Soviet arts administration very early on in the formation of the Bolshevik state, and their success at networking kept them in power for some time afterward. But their very success led to their eventual downfall. Over time, the network of modernists came to be *perceived* as having monopolized the leading positions of patronage and distribution of resources (whether themselves, or through their high-placed patrons). Consequently, the increasingly frequent and angry attacks against them by other groups (who were supported by other patrons within the Soviet arts administration) were inseparable

Figure 13. Kazimir Malevich, *Landscape with Five Houses*. About 1928. Oil on canvas. 83 × 62 cm. State Russian Museum.

from material considerations and structural/institutional issues underpinning them, and thus were not solely motivated by ideological or aesthetic differences.

The actual degree to which the modernists may have monopolized key positions of patronage and resource distribution, however, cannot be assumed a priori. Answering this question requires precisely the kind of detailed institutional investigation that I have attempted in each of the chap-

Figure 14. Kazimir Malevich, *Female Portrait.* About 1928. Oil on plywood. 58 × 49 cm. State Russian Museum.

ters of this book. Based on my analysis, it appears that the modernists in Moscow and Vitebsk acted in a much more competitive manner than they did in Petrograd/Leningrad; for in Moscow and Vitebsk they attempted and frequently succeeded in dominating patronage networks and the all-important access to scarce resources. However, the fact that the same group of people (the UNOVIS network) adopted a less clannish manner in a different institutional context suggests, of course, that this clannishness was not something inherent to vanguard artists. Rather, Malevich and his colleagues learned from their earlier experience and sought not to make the same mistake twice. Of course, this did not prevent representatives of other art groups from branding the State Institute of Artistic Culture a "state-sponsored monastery." Nor did it prevent members of this institute from seeing themselves as a besieged "citadel." However, a comparison of the three institutions that form the subject of this book suggests that in Leningrad, the attacks against the modernists were much more ideologically motivated, rather than based on objections to modernist artists' access to state resources and patrons. This book's emphasis on the institutional context in which the modernists found themselves is warranted by the fact that in the Soviet period the production, teaching, display, and consumption of art became a state-sponsored activity. Unlike in contemporary western Europe, with its functioning private art market, Soviet modernists had no other patrons except those embedded in various state agencies. Consequently, even though Russian modern art was heavily informed by European modernism, especially in its French, Italian, and German varieties, the structural transformation of the public sphere in postrevolutionary Russia created a set of unique conditions that unavoidably set Russian modernist artists apart from their counterparts elsewhere.[10] Paying attention to this difference, without essentializing it, is crucial for understanding the specificity of the Russian case and for making any kind of comparative statements about the various strands of European modernism. Indeed, this study about the role of artists and intellectuals under conditions of state patronage not only provides a counterargument to Peter Bürger's theory about the necessity of an autonomous avant-garde, but also extends beyond the world of art and into the wider discussion of the role of patronage networks in the rise, evolution, and decline of one-party-state systems.[11]

Although it is possible to make a case for Soviet exceptionalism in the art world, we must remember that survival, stability, and self-fashioning are integral to a successful career of any artist, regardless of political and economic contexts. Attention to artists' various strategies, including self-fashioning, has found expression in recent art historical studies.[12] The results of these kinds of inquiries have not been financial and aesthetic denigration of artists' productions, but a more comprehensive understanding of how their identities and circumstances shape their artistic choices. This book has attempted to make the same argument for Soviet modernists. The approach advocated in this book sidesteps the need to judge to what extent modernist artists like Malevich were true believers or were just donning Soviet masks. Ultimately all the artists under examination in this study participated in the discursive process of Soviet state-building.

Nevertheless, there were real institutional and ideological limits to modernist self-fashioning and the "sovietization" of Russian modernism. Despite the support of his friends within the arts administration, for example, Malevich's 1929 exhibition clearly did not convince everyone that he was a Soviet artist, for the very next year, the founder of Suprematism spent two months in jail, "being questioned about the ideological and political aspects of his art."[13] In 1934, however, Malevich did manage to survive the "Kirov flood," when 40,000 Leningraders, primarily *intelligenty* and white-collar workers, were arrested as "enemies of the people" and executed by Stalin's secret police on trumped-up charges of being involved in the assassination of Sergei Kirov, Leningrad's popular party boss. This narrow escape, as well as the opportunities afforded by the state-sponsored cult of Kirov, may explain why Malevich hoped to make a memorial bust in honor of the slain Communist, a choice of subject matter that would be politic for a modernist artist to undertake on the eve of the Great Purges.[14] And yet we must remember that with the most notable exceptions of Vera Ermolaeva,[15] Alexander Drevin,[16] and Nikolai Punin,[17] very few modernist artists were swept into the whirlwind of the Gulag, a fact that supports the contention that most modern artists who remained in the country successfully presented a sufficiently "sovietized" type of art,[18] and whose self-presentation met the demands for a "sovietized" intelligentsia: Rodchenko continued to use photography as his primary medium through the 1930s, and then returned to painting, albeit in a representational visual idiom; Tatlin found refuge working in the theater and lived until May 1953; N. Suetin (Malevich's student in Vitebsk and colleague at GINKhUK) was in charge of the Soviet pavilion devoted to "Art and Technology in Contemporary Life" at the International Exposition in Paris 1937; David Shterenberg returned to painting and in the early 1930s focused on works that reflected the demands for Socialist Realist painting, such as the *Brigade on Break,* from 1931; Natan Al'tman, who from 1920 to 1928 worked as a stage designer for the Jewish State Theatre in Moscow, had a solo exhibition in Leningrad in 1926. Al'tman moved to Paris in 1928, but returned to Leningrad and found a home in the theater, and lived until he was 81 years of age; Pyotr Vil'yams spent the 1930s and 1940s as a theater designer in Moscow, and died in Moscow in 1947. Kazimir Malevich was given a state funeral when he died of cancer in 1935.

This book ends with an examination of Malevich because I believe his case offers a good illustration of the way in which modernist artists were able to retain some agency into the late 1920s, and remain actors in the cultural sphere, albeit not entirely on their own terms, well into the 1930s and 1940s. His example encapsulates and summarizes the general story of

Russian modernists' engagement with the Bolshevik state and helps us to understand, not judge, their constant need to prove, both to their superiors in the arts administration and to themselves, that they were productive members of the Soviet intelligentsia. In our attempts to understand how Soviet ideology, practice, and discourse inflected Russian modernist art, we must acknowledge not only the political, economic, ideological, and institutional context in which this process took place, but also the self-conscious discursive and practical activities that allowed modernist artists to succeed for as long as they did under an increasingly repressive regime. Doing so removes the possible moral opprobrium associated with charges of political opportunism, sidesteps the dichotomy between inward belief and external compliance, and opens up new vistas in the study of the modern artist working within a system of state patronage.

NOTES

Introduction

1. See, for example, Mark Antliff, *Avant-Garde Fascism: The Mobilization of Myth, Art, and Culture in France, 1909–1939* (Durham, N.C.: Duke University Press, 2007); and Patricia Leighten, *Re-Ordering the Universe: Picasso and Anarchism, 1897–1914* (Princeton, N.J.: Princeton University Press, 1989). For American artists, see Andrew Hemingway, *Artists on the Left: American Artists and the Communist Movement, 1926–1956* (New Haven, Conn.: Yale University Press, 2002). For recent publications on Soviet artists and politics, see Christina Kiaer's award-winning *Imagine No Possessions: The Socialist Objects of Russian Constructivism* (Cambridge, Mass.: MIT Press, 2005), in which the author interprets Constructivist objects through the lens of socialist discourses and psychoanalytic theory, while Maria Gough's *Artist as Producer: Russian Constructivism in Revolution* (Berkeley: University of California Press, 2005) refocuses our attention on the roots of Constructivism and its engagement with socialist modernity.

2. Paul Wood, "The Politics of the Avant-Garde," in *The Great Utopia: The Russian and Soviet Avant-Garde, 1915–1932* (New York: Guggenheim Museum, 1992), 3.

3. Katerina Clark, "The 'Quiet Revolution' in Soviet Intellectual Life," in *Russia in the Era of NEP*, ed. Sheila Fitzpatrick, Alexander Rabinowitch, and Richard Stites (Bloomington: Indiana University Press, 1993), 211.

4. For more on the concept of self-fashioning, see Stephen Greenblatt, *Renaissance Self-Fashioning* (Chicago: University of Chicago Press, 2005).

5. Stephen Kotkin, *Magnetic Mountain: Stalinism as a Civilization* (Berkeley: University of California Press, 1997), 21–22.

6. See Aaron Cohen, *Imagining the Unimaginable: World War, Modern Art, and the Politics of Public Culture in Russia, 1914–1917* (Lincoln: University of Nebraska Press, 2008); and Jane Sharp, *Russian Modernism Between East and West: Natal'ia Goncharova and the Moscow Avant-Garde* (New York: Cambridge University Press, 2006).

7. For a detailed study of these early Soviet festivals, see James von Geldern, *Bolshevik Festivals: 1917–1920* (Berkeley: University of California Press, 1993).

8. For more on these dynamics between cultural institutions and the state, see György Péteri, ed., *Patronage, Personal Networks and the Party-State: Everyday Life in the Cultural Sphere in Communist Russia and East Central Europe* (Trondheim, Nor.: Norwegian University of Science and Technology, Program on East European Cultures and Societies, 2004).

9. The New Economic Policy (NEP) was introduced in 1921 and was designed to allow limited capitalist activity to boost the economy, which was in ruins after the Civil War and "War Communism." In particular, the NEP was aimed at appeasing the peasantry, by allowing individual peasants to sell surplus produce on the open market. For more on the NEP, see Alec Nove, *The Soviet Economic System* (Boston: Allen and Unwin, 1986).

10. Wood, "The Politics of the Russian Avant-Garde," 3.

11. Two recent studies that address this point are Martha Weitzel Hickey, *The Writer in Petrograd and the House of the Arts* (Evanston, Ill.: Northwestern University Press, 2009); and Marc Junge, *Die Gesellschaft ehemaliger politischer Zwangsarbeiter und Verbannter in der Sowjetunion: Gründung, Entwicklung und Liquidierung (1921–1935)* (Berlin: Akademie Verlag, 2009).

12. For example, Katerina Clark, in her essay "The 'Quiet Revolution,'" refutes the paradigm of alleged liberalism and political relaxation during the NEP, and convincingly argues that "sovietization," on an individual and an institutional level, had occurred by 1922. In the same vein, Michael David-Fox examines literature and censorship in "Glavlit, Censorship and the Problem of Party Policy in Cultural Affairs, 1922–28," *Soviet Studies* 44 (1992): 1045–68. Similarly, Stuart Finkel has recently argued that by 1923 "institutions of state control and practices of power that would thenceforth characterize the Soviet system had been established." Stuart Finkel, *On the Ideological Front: The Russian Intelligentsia and the Making of the Soviet Public Sphere* (New Haven, Conn.: Yale University Press, 2007), 227. Christopher Read, in *Culture and Power in Revolutionary Russia: The Intelligentsia and the Transition from Tsarism to Communism* (New York: St. Martin's, 1990), rejects the notion that the NEP era (1921–28) was a period of liberalism and describes the political, ideological, and financial constraints placed on the creative intelligentsia which paved the way for the implementation of a hegemonic culture in the late 1920s. He convincingly argues that the apparatus of cultural control had been established between 1920 and 1922 and steadily increased its power throughout the 1920s. Read concludes that the Central Committee's 1932 ban of all independent art groups and assertion of complete state control over artistic activity was but a reassertion of what had been in practice since 1920–22. See also Roger Pethybridge, *One Step Backward, Two Steps Forward: Soviet Society and Politics in the New Economic Policy* (Oxford: Clarendon, 1990).

13. Sheila Fitzpatrick, *Everyday Stalinism: Ordinary Life in Extraordinary Times: Soviet Russia in the 1930s* (Oxford: Oxford University Press, 1999), 109–14. Also see Sheila Fitzpatrick, "Intelligentsia and Power: Client-Patron Relations in Stalin's Russia," in *Stalinismus vor dem zweiten Weltkrieg: Neue Wege der Forschung,* ed. Manfred Hildermeier (Munich: R. Oldenbourg Verlag, 1998), 35–53.

14. See Daniel Orlovsky, "Political Clientelism in Russia: The Historical Perspective," in *Leadership Selection and Patron-Client Relations in the USSR and Yugoslavia, Selected Papers from the Second World Congress for Soviet and East European Studies,* ed. T. H. Rigby and Bohdan Harasymiw (London: Allen and Unwin, 1983).

15. The term "network" is aptly defined by Barbara Walker, in her study of Maximilian Voloshin and Soviet literary circles, as being made up of educated professionals who formed "personal bonds that were essentially pragmatic, not idealistic, calculated not unmediated, self-interested rather than self-sacrificial." These networks formed in the Soviet era in many ways drew "on the longstanding Russian elite tradition of network and patronage relations." Barbara Walker, *Maximilian Voloshin and the Russian Literary Circle: Culture and Survival in Revolutionary Times* (Bloomington: Indiana University Press, 2005), 8, 13.

16. For more on the "family circle," see Merle Fainsod, *Smolensk Under Soviet Rule* (Cambridge, Mass.: Harvard University Press, 1958), 48.

17. "Russian Futurism" had its roots in, but differed fundamentally from, Italian Futurism. Artists Vladimir and David Burliuk and Ilya Zdanevich were associated

with Russian Futurism, and David Burliuk (Vladimir died in 1917 in World War 1) and Zdanevich left Moscow shortly after the Revolution and were not associated with the "Futurists" after the Revolution.

18. The term "avant-garde" was not used to describe artistic activity in twentieth-century Russia until the 1960s in the West. See Éva Forgács, "How the New Left Invented East-European Art," *Centropa* 3 (May 2003): 93–104.

19. "Formalist" was another term used by Soviet art critics at the time, primarily as a form of abuse, to decry Futurist "nonobjective" and therefore "contentless" work as "alien" to the masses and Soviet ideology. The term originated due to the Futurists' association with the Formalist literary critic Viktor Shklovsky, who occasionally contributed to the Futurist organ *Art of the Commune* (*Iskusstvo kommuny*) in 1919.

20. For a detailed examination of the origins of this museum, see Svetlana Dzhafarova, "The Creation of the Museum of Painterly Culture," in *The Great Utopia: The Russian and Soviet Avant-Garde 1915–1932* (New York: Guggenheim Museum, 1992), 474–81. For a theoretical treatment of the Museum of Painterly Culture, see Maria Gough, "Futurist Museology," *Modernism/Modernity* 10 (April 2003).

21. See the careful scholarship of Aleksandra Shatskikh, especially *Vitebsk: The Life of Art,* trans. Katherine Foshko Tsan (New Haven, Conn.: Yale University Press, 2007). For archival documents relating to the Vitebsk school of art, see Irina Karasik, ed., *V kruge Malevicha: Soratniki, ucheniki, posledovateli v Rossii 1920–1950-kh* (St. Petersburg: Palace Editions, 2000); and Irina Vakar, T. N. Mikhienko, and Kazimir Severinovich Malevich, *Malevich o sebe, Sovremenniki o Maleviche: Pis'ma, dokumenty, vospominaniia, kritika* (Moscow: RA, 2004). Both collections of published documents provide the research with ample documentation, but little critical analysis.

22. See also Elena Basner, ed., *Muzei v muzee: Russkii avangard iz kollektsii Muzeia khudozhestvennoi kul'tury v sobranii Gosudarstvennogo russkogo muzeia* (St. Petersburg: Palace Editions, 1998).

23. For an in-depth historiographic treatment of the literature of Russia's avant-garde, see Pamela Kachurin, "One Step Forward, Two Steps Back: The Retreat of the Avant-Garde in the Early Soviet Era" (Ph.D. diss., Indiana University, 1998).

Chapter One

1. Previous works have focused only on selected aspects or limited periods in the museum's history. For an essay on its origins, see Svetlana Dzhafarova, "The Creation of the Museum of Painterly Culture," in *The Great Utopia: The Russian and Soviet Avant-Garde 1915–1932* (New York: Guggenheim Museum, 1992), 474–81; for a detailed description of the last cohort to work at the Museum of Painterly Culture, see Charlotte Douglas, "Terms of Transition: The 'First Discussional Exhibition' and the Society of Easel Painters," ibid., 451–65. For a fascinating theoretical explication of the museum, see Maria Gough, "Futurist Museology," *Modernism/Modernity* 10 (April 2003): 327–48.

2. For scholarly treatments of A. V. Lunacharsky, see Sheila Fitzpatrick, *The Commissariat of Enlightenment: Soviet Organization of Education and the Arts Under Lunacharsky, October 1917–1921* (Cambridge: Cambridge University Press, 2002); Timothy O'Connor, *The Politics of Soviet Culture: Anatolii Lunacharsky* (Ann Arbor, Mich.: UMI Research Press, 1983); A. L. Tait, *Lunacharsky: Poet of the Revolution*

(1875–1907) (Birmingham: Department of Russian Language and Literature, University of Birmingham, 1984).

3. Officially founded in late January 1918, a mere three months after the Bolshevik takeover, the department had neither a budget nor employees until June 1918. See *Smeta dokhodov i raskhodov Narodnogo kommissariata po prosveshcheniiu na vtoroi polugodie 1919* (Moscow, 1919), 12.

4. A. V. Lunacharsky, *Ob izobrazitel'nom iskusstve,* vol. 1 (Moscow: Nauka, 1966), 408.

5. G. K. Lukomsky, *Khudozhnik i revoliutsiia 1917–1922* (Berlin: E. A. Gutnova, 1923), 11. Lukomsky worked within the Department of Fine Arts as a member of the Collegium on Museum Matters.

6. "Eshche o chrezvychainom naloge," *Bednota* (January 1, 1919): 2.

7. A. V. Lunacharsky, "Postanovlenie NKP ob obespechenii khudozhnikov masterskami," *Izvestiya VTsIK* (September 21, 1918), 1.

8. Nils Nilsson, *Art, Society, Revolution: Russia 1917–1921* (Stockholm: Almqvist and Wiksell International, 1979), 31. The group also included Natan Al'tman, Sergei Chekhonin, and Grigorii Yatmanov, who would later become a highly placed administrator within the Main Scientific Administration.

9. For an excellent and thorough explication of the "Futurists'" engagement with Bolshevism and Anarchism immediately after the revolution, see Nina Gurianova, *The Aesthetics of Anarchy: Art and Ideology in the Early Russian Avant-Garde* (Berkeley: University of California Press, 2012).

10. Pamela Kachurin, "Working (for) the State: Vladimir Tatlin's Career in Early Soviet Russia and the Origins of *The Monument to the Third International*," *Modernism/Modernity* 19, no. 1 (January 2012).

11. Although he was certainly a supporter of progressive social reform, and even suspected of "revolutionary activity" in his student days at Penza. Larissa Zhadova, *Tatlin* (New York: Rizzoli, 1988), 447.

12. In 1920, already after Tatlin's departure for Petrograd, the Moscow SVOMAS was renamed VKhUTEMAS.

13. Christina Lodder, *Russian Constructivism* (New Haven, Conn.: Yale University Press, 1983), 49. As Lodder points out, membership in the Collegium was in flux and it is unclear exactly who was a member at what time. The Petrograd Division of the Department of Fine Arts had its own Collegium, composed of Natan Al'tman, Peter Vaulin, Karev, Matveev, Chekhonin, Yatmanov, and the critic Nikolai Punin.

14. Gosudarstvennyi arkhiv Rossiiskoi Federatsii [hereafter, GARF], *fond* [f.] A-2306, *opis* [op.] 23, *delo* [d.] 7, *list* [l.] 35.

15. GARF, f. A-2306, op. 23, d. 7, l. 35.

16. For a detailed discussion of the Purchasing Commission see Pamela Kachurin, "Purchasing Power: The State as Art Patron in Early Soviet Russia," *Biuletyn Historii Sztuki* 60, nos. 1–2 (1998): 169–83. On the days when Tatlin's work was up for sale, he would be absent, so as to prevent the appearance of "favoritism."

17. Tsentral'nyi gosudarstvennyi arkhiv Saint Petersburga [hereafter TsGA SPB] f. 143, op. 4, d. 14, l. 27 obverse [ob].

18. GARF, f. A-2306, op. 23, d. 8, l. 353.

19. GARF, f. A-2306, op. 23, d. 27, l. 9.

20. *Smeta dokhodov i raskhodov narodnogo komissariata po prosveshcheniiu* (Moscow, 1919), 54 and following.

21. "Pokupka kartin v Moskve," *Zhizn' iskusstva* 30 (November 1918): 2.

22. D. Shterenberg and A. V. Lunacharsky, "Ot Otdela IZO," *Iskusstvo kommuny* 1 (December 7, 1918): 3.

23. Alexei Tolstoy, "Agony of the Russian Intelligentsia," *Struggling Russia* (October 25, 1919): 507. This letter was originally written in early 1919, but published in the United States in October 1919.

24. Rossiiskii Gosudarstvennyi arkhiv literatury i iskusstva [hereafter, RGALI], f. 665, op. 1, d. 3, l. 4. Maria Gough correctly observes that this declaration should be interpreted as a protest against the Museum Department within IZO, whose membership included conservative critics, scholars, and museum directors with whom many vanguard artists had clashed in the late imperial period, including Igor Grabar and Alexander Benois. What was at stake was nothing less than control of the Soviet art world. See Maria Gough, "Futurist Museology," *Modernism/Modernity* 10, no. 2 (2003): 327–48.

25. "Otkrytie," *Iskusstvo kommuny* 11 (February 19, 1919): 2.

26. Svetlana Dzhafarova, "The Creation of the Museum of Painterly Culture," 479.

27. G. I. Ilina, *Kul'turnoe stroitel'stvo v Petrograde Oktiabr 1917–1920gg* (Leningrad: Nauka, 1982), 188.

28. "Rech' Lunacharskogo," *Iskusstvo kommuny* 11 (February 19, 1919): 2.

29. A February 1919 article attests to the fact that "cold is greatly worrying our museum workers. The Russian Museum finds itself in a critical situation. . . [Narkompros] promises heat for the museum but promises cannot be realized. The temperature in the museum is low, guards sit all the time in coats. They are afraid that freezing temperatures will ruin the paintings. If the question about heating museums is not resolved . . . the museum will be forced to close, although this will not help the preservation of works. "Kholoda i iskusstvo," *Zhizn' iskusstva* 77 (February 13, 1919): 2.

30. Sergei Shchukin was a wealthy collector of modern French painting during the late imperial period. Much of his collection is currently on view at the Pushkin Museum of Fine Arts in Moscow and the State Hermitage Museum in St. Petersburg. For more on Shchukin and other art patrons, see Beverly Whitney Kean, *French Painters, Russian Collectors: The Merchant Patrons of Modern Art in Pre-Revolutionary Russia* (London: Hodder and Stoughton, 1994).

31. GARF, f. A-2306, op. 23. d. 50, 1. 1.

32. Ibid.

33. *KPSS vo glave kul'turnoi revoliutsii SSSR* (Moscow: Politizdat, 1972), 32.

34. Dzhafarova, "The Creation of the Museum of Painterly Culture," 478.

35. One of the first museums established in 1919 was the Petrograd Museum of Artistic Culture, which will be discussed in more detail in Chapter Three. This museum was founded as a branch of the Moscow Museum of Painterly Culture, but by 1920 the Petrograd museum had received credits worth two million rubles to acquire works of art for itself. RGALI, f. 665, op. 1, d. 5, 1. 9.

36. RGALI, f. 665, op. 1, d. 5, 1. 103.

37. RGALI, f. 665, op. 1, d. 5, 1. 9.

38. RGALI, f. 665, op. 1, d. 12, 1 4

39. RGALI, f. 665, op. 1, d. 5, 1. 18.

40. RGALI, f. 665, op. 1, d. 5, 1. 15.

41. Dzhafarova, "The Creation of the Museum of Painterly Culture," 478. Dzhafarova reproduces the entire list.

42. RGALI, f. 665, op. 1, d. 5, 1. 9.
43. Ibid.
44. A. Efros, "Bibliografiia," *Khudozhestvennaia zhizn'* 2 (January 1920): 22.
45. Vassily Kandinsky, "Muzei zhivopisnoi kul'tury," *Khudozhestvennaia zhizn'* 2 (January 1920): 18–20.
46. IZO *Spravochnik,* 116.
47. Viktor Friche, "O politike IZO Narkomprosa," *Tvorchestvo* 11–12 (1920): 26–28.
48. Richard Pipes, *Russia Under the Bolshevik Regime* (New York: A. A. Knopf, 1993), 326.
49. "Instructions of the Central Committee to Communists Working in Narkompros," in *V. I. Lenin, Collected Works* (Moscow: Progress, 1966), 120–21.
50. GARF, f. 1250, op. 1, d. 55, 1. 223.
51. M. N. Pokrovskii, "Akademicheskii tsentr 'Narkomprosa,'" *Narodnoe prosveshchenie* (March 20, 1921): 3. Pokrovskii was Lunacharsky's second in command, a renowned Soviet historian who fell victim to the purges in 1932.
52. GARF, f. A-2306, op. 2, d. 706, l. 94.
53. B. Pliuskin-Kronin, "K obrazovanyu glavnogo khudozhestvennogo komiteta," *Narodnoe prosveshchenie* (March 20, 1921): 73–77.
54. GARF, f. A-2306, op. 3, d. 56, 1. 35.
55. B. Pliuskin-Kronin, "K obrazovaniiu glavnogo khudozhestvennogo komiteta," *Narodnoe prosveshchennie* (March 20, 1921): 73–77.
56. *Vestnik otdela Izobrazitel'nikh iskusstv Narkompros* 1 (March 10, 1921): 4.
57. RGALI, f. 665, op. 1, d. 20, l. 117.
58. 0 degrees Celsius. RGALI, f. 665, op. 1, d. 20, 1. 94.
59. GARF, f. A-2307, op. 8, d. 154, l. 4.
60. A. Sidorov, "Muzei zhivopisnoi kul'tury," *Tvorchestvo* 1–3 (January–March 1921): 43–50.
61. *Sobranie uzakoneny i rasporiazheny Rabochego i Krest'ianskogo Pravitel'stva* 98 (1920), 540. For more on the VKhUTEMAS, see Christina Lodder, *Russian Constructivism,* and Christina Lodder, "The VKhUTEMAS and the Bauhaus," in *The Avant-Garde Frontier: Russia Meets the West, 1910–1930,* ed. Gail Harrison Roman and Virginia Hagelstein Marquardt (Gainesville: University Press of Florida, 1992).
62. RGALI, f. 665, op. 1, d. 2, 1. 123.
63. GARF, f. A-2307, op. 3, d. 209, l. 3.
64. GARF, f. A-2307, op. 4, d. 10, ll. 193–193ob. By May 1922 the Main Scientific Administration administered 5 academies, 38 scientific institutions, 301 museums, 56 scientific-artistic institutions, and 99 academic-scientific libraries with a total of 16,000 workers (TsGALI SPB, f. 244, op. 1, d. 9, l. 6).
65. GARF, f. A-2307, op. 8, d. 160, ll. 17–17ob.
66. GARF, f. A-2307, op. 8, d. 162, ll. 74–85.
67. GARF, f. A-2307, op. 4, d. 20, 1. 84.
68. RGALI, f. 665, op. 1, d. 28, 1. 131.
69. Boris Thomson, *Lot's Wife and the Venus of Milo: Conflicting Attitudes to the Cultural Heritage in Modern Russia* (Cambridge: Cambridge University Press, 1978), 8.
70. For detailed discussion of Rodchenko's activities in INKhUK and VKhUTEMAS, see Christina Lodder, *Russian Constructivism* (New Haven, Conn.: Yale University Press, 1983).

71. Gough, "Futurist Museology," 340.

72. Ibid.

73. Ibid.

74. GARF, A-2306, op. 1, d. 609, l. 2.

75. RGALI, f. 664, op. 1, d. 3, 1. 2.

76. RGALI, f. 665, op. 1, d. 27, l. 25.

77. RGALI, f. 664, op. 1, d. 12, l. 22. The Povarskaya Street locale was farther from the center of Moscow than the Volkhonka Street locale, but still quite centrally located.

78. RGALI, f. 665, op. 1, d. 27, ll. 39–41.

79. GARF, f. A-2307, op. 3, d. 209, l. 24.

80. GARF, f. A-2307, op. 3, d. 209, l. 25.

81. GARF, f. A-2307, op. 3, d. 209, l. 32.

82. "Chronology," in *Aleksandr Rodchenko* (New York: Museum of Modern Art, 1998), 304.

83. GARF, f. A-2307, op. 3, d. 209, l. 39.

84. Since the funds allotted to the museum by the Main Scientific Administration were clearly insufficient, in December 1922 and in January and February 1923, Rodionov demanded and received additional funds for the Museum of Painterly Culture from the Main Scientific Administration, to ease Rodchenko's replacement into his new role.

85. Vil'yams is best remembered for his work as a set designer for Soviet theater and opera. For more biographical information on Pyotr Vil'yams, see "Pyotr Vladimirovich Vil'yams," in *Khudozhniki Narodov SSSR: Biobibliograficheskii slovar', Tom 2* (Moscow: Iskusstvo, 1972), 273–74.

86. The New Economic Policy, initiated in March 1921, allowed institutions and individuals to generate funds and use them to support salaries and operations.

87. RGALI, f. 664, op. 1, d. 1, l. 81.

88. GARF, f. A-2307, op. 3, d. 209, ll. 71–71ob.

89. GARF, f. A-2307, op. 3, d. 209, l. 88ob. It is not altogether surprising that Communist-dominated RABIS should intervene on behalf of the MZhK. The Fine Arts subsection of RABIS had numerous modernist artists, including at one time Sofia Dymshits-Tolstaya and Nikolai Punin.

90. See Charlotte Douglas, "Terms of Transition: The *First Discussional Exhibition* and the Society of Easel Painters," in *The Great Utopia: The Russian and Soviet Avant-Garde, 1915–1932* (New York: Guggenheim Museum, 1992), 451–65.

91. RGALI, f. 664, op. 1, d. 4, 1. 95. The museum had moved back to its former location on Volkhonka.

92. GARF, f. A-2307, op. 8, d. 133, 1. 51.

93. GARF, f. A-2307, op. 3, d. 209, l. 87.

94. GARF, f. A-2307, op. 3, d. 209, l. 84. The Main Scientific Administration complied with their request.

95. GARF, f. A-2307, op. 3, d. 209, 1.86.

96. GARF, f. A-2307, op. 3, d. 209, ll. 90–91. It is unclear whether these sales took place, or which paintings were considered "undesirable."

97. GARF, f. A-2307, op. 3, d. 210, 1. 5. Glavmuzei was the new name for the Department of Preservation, and it managed all museums in the country including historical museums, other art museums, and estates. The Department of Preservation

became the Main Museum Administration in July 1921, during the first Narkompros reorganization, and was placed under the management of the Academic Center. It became an independent administration under the Main Scientific Administration upon the dissolution of the Academic Center. In April 1923, the head of the Main Museum Administration wrote to the director of the Main Scientific Administration requesting the transfer of both the Museum of Painterly Culture and the Polytechnical Museum to its management.

98. RGALI, f. 664, op. 1, d. 4, 1. 8. Lazar Vainer is described by Charlotte Douglas as a "genteel 38 year old sculptor who before World War I had attended the École des Beaux-Arts in Paris" (Douglas, "Terms of Transition," 453). For more information on Vainer, see "Lazar Yakovlevich Vainer," in *Khudozhniki Narodov SSSR: Biobibliograficheskii slovar', Tom 2* (Moscow: Iskusstvo, 1972), 146. Undoubtedly Vainer was appointed as head to redress the lack of Communists working in the art world.

99. GARF, f. A-2307, op. 8, d. 182, 1. 14. Grabar' was laid off from Glavmuzei in early May 1923 (GARF, f. A-2307, op. 8, d. 182, 1. 82).

100. GARF, f. A-2306, op. 69, d. 737, ll. 7–7ob.

101. GARF, f. A-2307, op. 3, d. 209, l. 95.

102. GARF, f. A-2307, op. 3, d. 209, l. 96.

103. GARF, f. A-2307, op. 3, d. 210, l. 8.

104. RGALI, f. 664, op. 1, d. 11, l. 220.

105. RGALI, f. 664, op. 1, d. 4, l. 2.

106. GARF, f. A-2307, op. 3, d. 210, l. 2.

107. RGALI, f. 664, op. 1, d. 8, l. 25.

108. Although working in different groups, the three dissolved their respective groups and formed the Society of Easel Painters (OST).

109. Nikritin, although he was not a member of OST, did attempt to find a type of realism—some say unsuccessfully—suitable to the new Soviet context.

110. Douglas, "Terms of Transition," 453.

111. RGALI, f. 664, op. 1, d. 4, 1. 20.

112. RGALI, f. 664, op. 1, d. 10, 1. 54. In June 1918 the Tretyakov Gallery, which held the largest collection of Russian art assembled by the wealthy industrialist Pavel Tretyakov, was nationalized by state decree. The decree read, in part: "Because of its cultural and artistic significance . . . the interests of the working classes demand that the Tretyakov Gallery be administered by the Commissariat of Enlightenment" (Rossiiskaya SFSR, 1917, *Sobranie uzakonenii rasporyazhenii Rabochego i Krest'ianskogo Pravitel'stva,* 485). Pavel Tretyakov had donated the museum to the city of Moscow in the 1890s. For more on the process of nationalization and requisition of private property, see Sean McMeekin, *History's Greatest Heist: The Looting of Russia by the Bolsheviks* (New Haven, Conn.: Yale University Press, 2009).

113. *Narodnoe prosveshchenie v RSFSR k 1925/1926 uchebnom godu (otchet Narkomprosa RSFSR za 1924/1925)* (Moscow, 1926), 213–18. The Museum of Proletarian Culture was annexed to the Tretyakov Gallery in spring 1924 (GARF, f. A-2307, op. 9, d. 204, 1. 140).

114. RGALI, f. 665, op. 1, d. 27, ll. 131–32.

115. GARF, f. A-2306, op. 69, d. 141, ll. 2–5. This ruling was issued by the Scholarly Council within the Main Scientific Administration.

116. RGALI, f. 664, op. 1, d. 12, 1. 21.

117. At the start of the 1925–26 fiscal year, for example, all of MZhK's expen-

ditures had to be approved by the Tretyakov Board of Directors before funds were allotted; and the Tretyakov threatened to withhold salaries if expenditures were made without their approval (RGALI, f. 664, op. 1, d. 8, 1. 23). Although Vainer was also elected to the Scholarly Council of the Tretyakov Gallery, he was no longer considered the director of the Museum of Painterly Culture, but merely the chief curator (*khranitel'*), with Vil'yams acting the part of the assistant curator of the collection (RGALI, f. 664, op. 1, d. 10, 1. 30).

118. RGALI, f. 664, op. 1, d. 12, l. 165.

119. RGALI, f. 664, op. 1, d. 8, l. 23.

120. RGALI, f. 664, op. 1, d. 8, 1. 33.

121. RGALI, f. 664, op. 1, d. 11, ll. 165–67. Vil'yams did note that of those 3,733 visitors, 1,274 actually paid for admittance, while 2,459, presumably students, entered for free.

122. RGALI, f. 664, op. 1, d. 12, l. 71. Between October 1925 and March 1926, a full third of the museum's operating expenses was covered by its own income (RGALI, f. 664, op. 1, d. 10, l. 45).

123. RGALI, f. 664, op. 1, d. 11, ll. 165–67.

124. "L. Ya. Vainer," in *Khudozhniki narodov sssr,* 146. Vil'yams had also painted a portrait of Vainer.

125. A. D. Sarabianov, *Neizvestnyi Russkii Avangard v muzeiakh i chastnykh sobraniakh* (Moscow: Sovetskii Khudozhnik, 1992), 29.

126. RGALI, f. 664, op. 1, d. 13, l. 59.

127. GARF, f. A-2307, op. 10, d. 176, ll. 17–18.

128. RGALI, f. 664, op. 1, d. 11, l. 167.

129. It is not clear what connection, if any, the relocation of the MZhK had with the near-simultaneous reorganization of the Tretyakov Gallery, which lost its non-Russian collections to the Museum of Fine Arts in Moscow (formerly the Rumyantsev Museum) and was renamed, albeit temporarily, the Main Museum of Russian Art in 1926.

130. The MZhK relocated to the site of the former Polytechnical Museum on Ilynsky Street in September 1928—a move tinged with some irony, since the Polytechnical Museum was the site of some of the more vociferous artistic debates and proclamations staged by the members of Russia's late-imperial avant-garde. RGALI, f. 664, op. 1, d. 1, l. 187.

131. RGALI, f. 664, op. 1, d. 13, 1. 2 and f. 664, op. 1, d. 13, 1. 39.

132. RGALI, f. 664, op. 1, d. 13, 1. 36. I was unable to locate an exhibition catalog, or a list of what was on view at the Museum of Painterly Culture.

133. For a capsule biography, see *1917: Chastnye svidetel'stva o revoliutsii v pis'makh Lunacharskogo i Martova,* ed. N. S. Antonova and L. A. Rogovaia (Moscow: Izd-vo Rossiiskogo universiteta druzhby narodov, 2005). Kristi was arrested in 1937 during the Great Purges, but survived incarceration.

134. RGALI, f. 664, op. 1, d. 13, 1. 3.

135. RGALI, f. 664, op. 1, d. 12, l. 224.

136. RGALI, f. 664, op. 1, d. 13, 1. 59.

137. Although the Tretyakov Gallery was informed in 1928 that it must ensure permanent accommodations for the museum in its present location. RGALI, f. 664, op. 1, d. 13, 1. 55.

138. RGALI, f. 645, op. 1, d. 4, l. 1.

139. RGALI, f. 664, op. 1, d. 12, ll. 223–24. See Alfred Evans, *Soviet Marxism-Leninism: The Decline of an Ideology* (Westport, Conn.: Praeger, 1993).

140. RGALI, f. 664, op. 1, d. 12, l. 223.

Chapter Two

1. The Vitebsk People's Art School is sometimes called the Vitebsk Free Art Studios (VitSvomas).

2. The Vitebsk region (*guberniia*) was still a part of the RSFSR in 1919. It became part of the Byelorussian Soviet Socialist Republic in 1924.

3. On Ermolaeva, see E. F. Kovtun, M. M. Babanazarova, and E. D. Gazieva, *Avangard, ostanovlennyi na begu* (Leningrad: Aurora, 1989); E. F. Kovtun, "Khudozhnitsa knigi V. M. Ermolaeva," *Iskusstvo knigi,* no. 8 (1975): 68–79; A. Zainchkovskaia, T. Goriacheva, and L. Vostretsova, *Vera Ermolaeva, 1893–1937* (St. Petersburg: Palace Editions, 2008); Antoniny Zainchkovskoi, *Vera Ermolaeva, 1893–1937* (Moscow: Galeev Galereia: Skorpion, 2009).

4. "The first systematic school of abstract painting in the modern movement." Camilla Gray, *The Russian Experiment in Art, 1863–1922,* revised and enlarged by Marian Burleigh-Motley (London: Thames and Hudson, 1986), 141. Charlotte Douglas's 1991 definition of Suprematism still stands as the most lucid: the geometric forms on white backgrounds functioned as "contemplative images," aids in attaining an evolved state of mind, freed from rationality and logic, or a *zaum* state. Charlotte Douglas, "Biographical Outline," in *Malevich: Artist and Theoretician* (New York: Flammarion, 1991), 10–12.

5. Clark, "The 'Quiet Revolution,'" 217.

6. A. Shatskikh, *Vitebsk: The Life of Art,* trans. Katherine Foshko Tsan (New Haven, Conn.: Yale University Press, 2007), 15.

7. Ibid., 22. Chagall had lived in Paris in 1911–14, returned to Vitebsk at the outbreak of World War I, and then in 1915 moved to Petrograd, where he remained until September 1918. For a detailed explication of Chagall's activities during his two years in Vitebsk, see A. Shatskikh, "Poslednie vitebskiie gody Mark Shagala," in *Shagalovskitsi Sbornik* (Vitebsk: N. A. Pankov, 1996), 245–55.

8. Ziva Amishai-Maisels, "Chagall and the Jewish Revival: Center or Periphery?" in *Tradition and Revolution: The Jewish Renaissance in Russian Avant-Garde Art, 1912–1928,* ed. Ruth Apter-Gabriel (Jerusalem: Israel Museum, 1987), 85.

9. Ibid.

10. A. Podlipskii. *Mark Shagal: Osnovnye daty zhizni i tvorchestva* (Vitebsk: Dommuzei Marka Shagala, 1993), 9.

11. For a detailed analysis of *Iskusstvo kommuny,* see Christina Lodder, "Art of the Commune: Politics and Art in Soviet Journals, 1917–20," *Art Journal* 52 (1993): 24–33.

12. Marc Chagall, "Pis'mo iz Vitebska," *Iskusstvo kommuny* 3 (December 22, 1918): 1.

13. W. Bruce Lincoln, *Red Victory: A History of the Russian Civil War* (New York: Simon and Schuster, 1989), 364; Diane P. Koenker, "Urbanization and Deurbanization in the Russian Revolution and Civil War," in *Party, State, and Society in the Russian Civil War: Explorations in Social History,* ed. Diane P. Koenker, William G. Rosenberg, and Ronald Grigor (Bloomington: Indiana University Press, 1989), 81.

14. Russian Museum Manuscript Department, f. 100, d. 249, l. 67 (reminiscences of Sophia Dymshits-Tolstaya).

15. I. Bruk, "Mark Shagal i Aleksandr Romm: K publikatsii pisem M. Shagala k A. Rommu (1910–1915) i vospominanii A. Romma 'Mark Shagal' (1944)," *Iskusstvoznanie* 2 (2003): 569–87.

16. For more on Ivan Puni's and Ksenia Boguslavskaya's roles in Vitebsk, see Shatskikh, *Vitebsk: The Life of Art,* 31 and following.

17. Nikolai Gugnin, "Iz istorii Vitebskoi khudozhestvennoi shkoli," in *Shagalovskitsi Sbornik,* 108. Thanks to Ernest Zitser for bringing this source to my attention.

18. Shatskikh, *Vitebsk: The Life of Art,* 104.

19. Ibid., 38–39.

20. Ibid., 60.

21. A. Shatskikh, "K. Malevich v Vitebske," *Iskusstvo* 2 (1988): 38–43. However, as Shatskikh notes, Malevich was planning only a brief sojourn in Vitebsk, before a planned move to Petrograd in 1920 where he already had a network of friends and supporters in place (Shatskikh, *Vitebsk: The Life of Art,* 93).

22. Bruk, "Mark Shagal i Aleksandr Romm," 569–87.

23. A. Romm, "O muzeinom stroitel'stve i Vitebskom muzei sovremennogo iskusstva," *Iskusstvo* 1 (March 1921): 6.

24. Shatskikh, *Vitebsk: The Life of Art,* 93.

25. Shatskikh, "K. Malevich v Vitebske," 38. See Kazimir Malevich, *O novykh sistemakh v iskusstve, statika i skorost', ustanovlenie* (Vitebsk, R.S.F.S.R.: Rabota i izdanie arteli khudozhestvennogo truda pri Vitsvomase, 1919). For an English translation, see K. S. Malevich, "On New Systems of Art," trans. Xenia Glowacki-Prus and Arnold McMillin, edited by Troels Andersen, in *Essays on Art, 1915–1933* (London: Rapp and Whiting, 1969).

26. Shatskikh, "K. Malevich v Vitebske," 39.

27. Lev Yudin, a student in the school, enthused: "How strong is this K[azimir] S[everinovich]. When our people [at the People's School of Art] began to wail and complain about the high prices [of food and life in Vitebsk] and it seemed really as if the world was going under, K[azimir] S[everinovich] arrived and straightaway everyone adopted a different frame of mind. He spread a different atmosphere around him, he is certainly the leader." Susan Compton, *Chagall* (London: Royal Academy of Arts in association with Weidenfeld and Nicolson, 1985), 72.

28. For a detailed description of the sequence of events relating to the formation of UNOVIS, see Catherine Cooke, "From Theory into Teaching," *Art & Design* 5, nos. 5–6 (1989): 6–31; and Shatskikh, *Vitebsk: The Life of Art.*

29. Shatskikh, "K. Malevich v Vitebske," 41.

30. A. Shatskikh, "Chagall and Malevich in Vitebsk: A History of Their Relations," *Bulletin AICARC* 1–2 (1989): 7–10. After Dobuzhinksky's departure in the spring of 1919, Chagall was the director of the school until his departure in June 1920.

31. In the existing historiography, the term "coup" is used to refer to the sudden departure of Chagall, who left Vitebsk supposedly because of Malevich's machinations. However, the existing evidence also supports the conclusion that Malevich stepped into the power vacuum created by the departure of the disillusioned Dobuzhinsky, who decided to leave his position as director of the People's School of Art to devote more time to his own work, and eventually emigrated from the Soviet Union. See Shatskikh, "Chagall and Malevich in Vitebsk"; and Shatskikh, *Vitebsk: A Life in Art.*

32. Shatskikh, *Vitebsk: A Life in Art,* 311.

33. From this perspective, Suprematism as a creative strategy was meant to serve as an antidote to the horrors of war in 1919–20, much as it did when it was first formulated in 1915. As Aaron Cohen has argued, when it was introduced in 1915, Suprematism provided an antidote to the grisly reality of the First World War. See Aaron Cohen, *Imagining the Unimaginable: World War, Modern Art, and the Politics of Public Culture in Russia, 1914–1917* (Lincoln: University of Nebraska Press, 2009), 144. For a discussion of how the continuous unrest at the beginning of the twentieth century shaped Russian politics, see Peter Holquist, *Making War, Forging Revolution: Russia's Continuum of Crisis, 1914–1921* (Cambridge, Mass.: Harvard University Press, 2002).

34. Shatskikh, *Vitebsk: The Life of Art,* 149.

35. Ibid., 125

36. Larissa Zhadova, *Malevich: Suprematism and Revolution in Russian Art 1910–1930* (New York: Thames and Hudson, 1982), 54.

37. Ibid., 91.

38. This instance of making art education Soviet is equivalent to the proletarianization of Russian universities, beginning in the 1920s. See Igal Halfin, "The Construction of the Workers' Intelligentsia: 'Proletarianization' of Soviet Universities in the 1920s" (Ph.D. diss., Columbia University, 1994, 2 vols.).

39. Catherine Cooke, "Malevich: From Theory into Teaching," 14–15.

40. For a reproduction of the entire Communist Party questionnaire of 1920, see V. I. Lenin, *Polnoe sobranie sochinenii,* vol. 41 (Moscow: God. Izdatel'stvo Politicheskoi Literatury, 1962), 465–68.

41. A. Shatskikh in *Vitebsk: The Life of Art* describes this "injection of political phraseology" as a "concession to the spirit of the times" (109).

42. Official statutes in Vakar et al., *Malevich o sebe, Sovremenniki o Maleviche: Pis'ma, dokumenty, vospominaniia, kritika* (Moscow: RA, 2004), 442–44.

43. Shatskikh, *Vitebsk: The Life of Art,* 109.

44. Ibid., 218.

45. This document is reproduced in full in Vakar et al., *Malevich o sebe,* 1:442–44.

46. In her publication of this document, A. Lisova comments that although it was signed by Ivan Gavris, the future rector of the Vitebsk School of Art, "Malevich undoubtedly took a leading role in the formulation of the document." Vakar et al., *Malevich o sebe,* 1:443.

47. Only five members of UNOVIS eventually joined the Communist Party and formed a separate fraction, and all of them were students. Shatskikh, *Vitebsk: The Life of Art,* 49.

48. See, for example, Martha Hickey, *The Writer in Petrograd and the House of the Arts* (Evanston, Ill.: Northwestern University Press, 2009). The author shows that the literary intelligentsia—albeit a small network of writers and its audience—were seen as a threat to the state.

49. For a full discussion of independent organizations in the early Soviet era, and their fate, see Stuart Finkel, *On the Ideological Front: The Russian Intelligentsia and the Making of the Soviet Public Sphere* (New Haven, Conn.: Yale University Press, 2007), 4.

50. Shatskikh, *Vitebsk: The Life of Art,* 142–43.

51. On "agit-trains," see Peter Kenez, *The Birth of the Propaganda State* (New York: Cambridge University Press, 1985), 58–62.

52. K. Malevich, "Opartii v iskusstve," *Put' UNOVISA,* no. 1 (Vitebsk, 1921), 1.

53. M. Kunin, "Partiinost' v iskusstve," *UNOVIS Almanac,* no. 2 (Vitebsk, 1921), 2–8.

54. Cooke, "From Theory into Teaching," 7–27.

55. Shatskikh, "Chagall and Malevich in Vitebsk: A History of Their Relations," 7–10.

56. Ilya Chashnik, "Unovis: Leaflet of the Creative Committee," no. 1, November 20, 1920, reprinted in Zhadova, *Malevich,* 299.

57. "Working Schedule of the Council," reprinted in Zhadova, *Malevich,* 317.

58. Vakar et al., *Malevich o sebe,* 1:138–39. Ivan Alekseevich Kudryashov (1896–1970) was a painter, graphic artist, and teacher in the Moscow Free Art Studios. He organized the Orenburg branch of UNOVIS.

59. Shatskikh, "K. Malevich v Vitebske," 40.

60. Ibid., 41. "War Communism" is the term applied to the period of the Russian Civil War (1918–20) which pitted a newly formed "Red Army" against a range of disparate military forces that were united by loyalty to the Tsar. "War Communism" was a combination of extremely harsh emergency measures and socialist dogma introduced by Lenin to combat the social and economic problems brought on by the Russian Civil War.

61. Komitet po bor'be s bezrabotnitsei—Vitebsk, 1919 (Committee for the Struggle with Unemployment). Reprinted in *Izdaniia perioda revoliutsii i grazhdanskoĭ voĭny (1917–1921) v Rossii: Katalog kollektsii* (Moscow: Biblioteka, 1991–94), part 3 (1919), 24.

62. See Pamela Kachurin, "One Step Forward, Two Steps Back: The Retreat of the Avant-Garde in the Early Soviet Era" (Ph.D. diss., Indiana University, 1998).

63. Shatskikh, *Vitebsk: The Life of Art,* 172.

64. Ibid. Sergei Kirov was the head of the Leningrad Communist Party when he was assassinated in 1933. The search for his assassins resulted in the "Kirov Flood" when 40,000 "enemies of the people" living in Leningrad were arrested and executed within several months.

65. V. V. Shamshur, *Prazdnestva revoliutsii: Organizatsiia i oformlenie sovetskikh massovykh torzhestv v Belorussii* (Minsk: Nauka i tekhnika, 1989), 49. Malevich probably did not come up with this slogan himself, as the slogans to be used in the festivals were determined by the Propaganda Department of the Central Committee and published in the local newspapers.

66. Lissitzky himself defined the Proun thusly: "Proun begins as a level surface, turns into a model of three-dimensional space, and goes on to construct all the objects of everyday life. In this way Proun goes beyond painting and the artist . . . and the machine and the engineer . . . and advances to the construction of space" (Sophie Lissitzky-Kuppers, *El Lissitzky: Life, Letters, Texts* [London: Thames and Hudson, 1980], 348).

67. See Kendall E. Bailes, *Technology and Society Under Lenin and Stalin: Origins of the Soviet Technical Intelligentsia, 1917–1941* (Princeton, N.J.: Princeton University Press, 1978); and Loren R. Graham, *Science in Russia and the Soviet Union: A Short History* (Cambridge, Mass.: Harvard University Press, 1993).

68. Jan F. Triska, *Soviet Communism: Programs and Rules* (San Francisco: Chandler, 1962), 143.

69. *KPSS v rezoliutsiakh i resheniakh s'ezdov konferentsii i plenumov TsK* (Moscow: Politizdat, 1954), 477 and following.

70. M. G. Braverman, "Tekushchii moment i professional'noe obrazovanie," *Narodnoe prosveshchenie* 59–61 (May 1, 1920): 3.

71. The notable exception is T. J. Clark, whose discussion of Lissitzky's signboard *Workbenches Await You* makes reference to production propaganda. See "God Is Not Cast Down," in *Farewell to an Idea: Episodes from a History of Modernism* (New Haven, Conn.: Yale University Press, 1999).

72. T. A. Remizova, *Kul'turno-prosvetitel'naya rabota v RSFSR, 1921–1925 gg* (Moscow: Akademii nauk SSSR, 1962), 179.

73. Ibid.

74. Vladimir Lenin, "Theses of Production Propaganda," in *Collected Works,* 45 vols. (Moscow: Progress, 1960–70), 31:404.

75. Remizova, *Kul'turno-prosvetitel'naya rabota v RSFSR,* 189 and following.

76. L. Khidekel, "UNOVIS in the Studios," *UNOVIS Almanac,* no. 2 (Vitebsk, 1921), trans. Cooke in "From Theory into Teaching," 29.

77. Shatskikh, *Vitebsk: The Life of Art,* 143. For more on Ilya Chashnik, see Karasik, ed., *V kruge Malevicha.*

78. Ilya Chashnik, "The Architectural and Technical Faculty," *UNOVIS Almanac,* no. 2 (Vitebsk, 1921).

79. Aleksandra Shatskikh dates this signboard to 1919–20. However, its function was clearly production propaganda, thus a date of 1920–21 is more likely.

80. Zhadova, *Malevich,* 86. The plan for students and faculty to engage in "laboratory work" also appears in the proposed curriculum for the academic year 1921–22.

81. Graham, *Science in Russia,* 174.

82. M. S. Bastrakova, *Stanovlenie sovetskoi sistemy organizatsii nauki 1917–1922* (Moscow: Nauka, 1973), 208.

83. Boris Thomson, *Lot's Wife and the Venus of Milo: Conflicting Attitudes to the Cultural Heritage in Modern Russia* (Cambridge: Cambridge University Press, 1978), 8.

84. Kazimir Malevich, *Ot kubizma i Futurisma k Suprematismu: Novyi zhivopisnyi realism,* 3rd ed. (Moscow: [s.n.], 1916), reproduced on one monochrome microfiche by Chadwyck-Healey, Cambridge, 1976, in the series "Russian Futurism 1910–1916: Poetry and Manifestos."

85. Zhadova, *Malevich,* 66.

86. Cooke, "From Theory into Teaching," 13.

87. "Programme of a United Audience in Painting of the Vitebsk State Free Workshops," UNOVIS Collective, trans. L. Zhadova, *Malevich,* 314. This unsigned article has been attributed to Malevich by Shatskikh (Shatskikh, *Vitebsk: The Life of Art,* 137).

88. Ibid., as reprinted in Zhadova, *Malevich,* 16.

89. Shatskikh, *Vitebsk: The Life of Art,* 137.

90. Most notably, Stephen Cohen has made this argument in *Bukharin and the Bolshevik Revolution: A Political Biography, 1888–1938* (New York: A. A. Knopf, 1973).

91. For more on the state- and party-imposed strictures on creative activities and the intelligentsia, see the cited publications by Stuart Finkel, Katerina Clark, and Christopher Read, http://library.duke.edu/catalog/search/recordid/DUKE000875471; Read, *Culture and Power in Revolutionary Russia;* and Marc Junge, *Gesellschaft ehemaliger politischer Zwangsarbeiter und Verbannter in der Sowjetunion: Gründung, Entwicklung und Liquidierung (1921–1935)* (Berlin: Akademie Verlag, 2009). Junge convincingly argues that during the era of the New Economic Policy (NEP), the Bolshevik leader-

ship imposed tighter restrictions on political, cultural, and social activity as a way of countering the "retreat" in the economic sphere.

92. Although the reorganization of Narkompros began in November 1920, the Vitebsk People's School of Art was still operating as it had been, with the same name and under IZO. The school's name changed to the Vitebsk Art-Practical Institute, under the control of the Main Administration of Professional Education, in April 1921 (GARF, f. A-2307, op. 4, d. 12, 1. 105).

93. A. Romm, "Vitebskaia gosudarstvennaia khud. masterskaia," *Iskusstvo* 2–3 (1921): 24.

94. Bruk, "Mark Shagal i Aleksandr Romm," 569–87.

95. A. Romm, "Vystavka v Vitebske 1921g.," *Iskusstvo* 4–6 (April–August 1921): 41.

96. "Ot redaktsii," *Iskusstvo* 1 (March 1921): 1.

97. An essay by Malevich simply entitled "UNOVIS" appeared in the first issue of *Iskusstvo.*

98. A. V. Lunacharsky, "Iskusstvo i revoliutsia," *Iskusstvo* 1 (March 1921): 2–3. Emphasis in the original.

99. A. Romm, "O muzeiinom stroitel'stvei Vitebskom muzei sovremennogo iskusstva," *Iskusstvo* 1 (March 1921): 6.

100. M. Kunin, "Ob Unovise," *Iskusstvo* 2–3 (1921): 14–16.

101. Peter Kenez, *A History of the Soviet Union from the Beginning to the End* (Cambridge: Cambridge University Press, 1999), 37.

102. John Milner, *A Dictionary of Russian and Soviet Artists, 1420–1970* (Woodbridge, U.K.: Antique Collector's Club, 1993), 457.

103. Ibid., 477.

104. Romm, "Vitebskaia gosudarstvennaia khud. masterskaia," 24.

105. GARF f. A-1565, op. 9, d. 32, 1. 15.

106. GARF, f. A-2307, op. 4, d. 12, 1. 105.

107. GARF, f. A-2307, op. 4, d. 12, 1. 106.

108. Other institutions now under the Vitebsk Gubprofobr Arts Sector were the art schools in Velizh and Polotsk, the Vitebsk State conservatory, the first stage and music school in Vitebsk, and music schools in Polotsk, Nevel, and Velizh. There was also a school called the Artistic-Workers Technical School in Vitebsk. These nine institutions had 456 students.

109. Gosudarstvennyi Arkhiv Vitebebskogo Oblast' (hereafter GAVO), f. 837, op. 1, d. 59, 1. 2. I was unable to determine the comparative rates of inflation for the cities and provinces, but it was not as sharp as in urban centers.

110. GAVO, f. 837, op. 1, d. 59, l. 26.

111. *Izvestiia* of June 2, 1921, reported that teachers' "salaries [in the Vitebsk region] are scarce and are paid unevenly . . . Rations are given out irregularly . . . [and teachers] are literally starving. Some are going to other institutions." *Izvestiia* 119 (June 2, 1921): 2.

112. GARF, f. 130, op. 5, d. 635, 1. 44.

113. M. Pokrovsky, "Doklad Glavprofobra," *Narodnoe prosveshchenie* 25 (October 1921): 21. VTsIK decreed that Glavprofobr was to close down some of the colleges and institutes by July 1922 (GARF, f. 1250, op. 1, d. 1, 1. 192).

114. GARF, f. A-1565, op. 3, d. 160, 1. 7.

115. V. Korablev, "Khudozhestvenno-professional'nie shkoly," *Zhizn' iskusstva* 27 (July 11, 1922): 1.

116. GARF, f. A-1565, op. 9, d. 116, ll. 4–6.
117. GAVO, f. 1319, op. 1, d. 1, l. 148.
118. GAVO, f. 1319, op.1, d. 1, l. 67.
119. GARF, f. A-1565, op. 2, d. 181, l. 2ob. On March 28, 1922, Shterenberg notified all art schools that it was necessary to begin charging students for the right to attend art institutes (GARF, f. A-2307, op. 4, d. 12, 1. 42).
120. GARF, f. A-1565, op. 3, d. 160, l. 5.
121. GARF, f. A-2306, op. 1, d. 459, ll. 4–9. Other closures during this year included the Vladikavkaz Polytechnical Institute, and universities in Orlov, Tambov, Simbirsk, and Kostroma.
122. GARF, f. A-1565, op. 9, d. 116, l. 3.
123. David Shterenberg, "Tesiz doklada OKhOBRa," *Biulleten' Glavrofobra* 25 (September 1921): 4–5.
124. GARF, f. A-1565, op. 9, d. 490, ll. 1–3.
125. Finkel, *On the Ideological Front,* 151.
126. For a complete description of the debate, see Vasilii Rakitin, "Malevich und INKhuK," in *Kasimir Malewitsch zum 100. Geburtstag* (Cologne: Galerie Gmurzynska, 1978).
127. A. Shatskikh, "UNOVIS: Epicenter of a New World," in *The Great Utopia: The Russian and Soviet Avant-Garde, 1915–1932* (New York: Guggenheim Museum, 1992), 62.
128. Malevich had been arrested, held briefly, and released in the summer of 1921. Shatskikh speculates that either his foreign-sounding name or his foreign correspondence led to his arrest (Shatskikh, *Vitebsk: The Life of Art,* 219).
129. Angelica Zander Rudenstine, *Russian Avant-Garde Art: The George Costakis Collection* (New York: Abrams, 1981), 88.
130. Shatskikh, "UNOVIS: Epicenter of a New World," 62.
131. Ibid.
132. TsGALI SPB, f. 244, op. 1, d. 2, 1. 3.
133. Shatskikh, *Vitebsk: The Life of Art,* 224.
134. GARF, f. A-2307, op. 3, d. 209, ll. 36–38.
135. The exceptions are Elvira Ershova's monograph *Istoricheskie sud'by khudozhestvennoi intelligentsii Belorussi 1917–1941* (Moscow, 1994); Gugnin, "Iz istorii Vitebskoi khudozhestvennoi shkoly"; and Shatskikh's *Vitebsk: The Life of Art.*
136. GARF, f. A-1565, op. 9, d. 379, 1. 7.
137. GARF, f. A-1565, op. 9, d. 379, 1. 33ob.
138. GARF, f. A-1565, op. 9, d. 379, 1. 19.
139. GARF, f. A-1565, op. 9, d. 379, 1. 15.
140. "Polozhenie o tekhnikumach," *Ezhenedel'nik Narkomprosa* 7 (July 28, 1923): 13–15.
141. GARF, f. A-1565, op. 9, d. 379, ll. 19–20.
142. Ershova, *Istoricheskie sud'by khudozhestvennoi intelligentsii,* 119.
143. Ibid.
144. GARF, f. A-1565, op. 9, d. 379, ll. 33–33ob.

Chapter Three

1. Szymon Bojko, "Study of the History of the Institute of Artistic Culture," in *Kasimir Malewitsch zum 100. Geburtstag* (Cologne: Galerie Gmurzynska, 1978); La-

rissa Zhadova, "Gosudarstvennyi institut khudozhestvennoi kul'tury v Leningrade," *Problemy istorii sovetskoi arkhitektury* 4 (1978): 25–28; Elena Basner et al., *Muzei v muzee: Russkii avangard iz kollektsii Muzeia khudozhestvennoi kul'tury v sobranii Gosudarstvennogo russkogo muzeia* (St. Petersburg: Palace Editions, 1998); Irina Karasik, "Muzei khudozhestvennoi kul'tury: Evolutsiia idei," in *Russkii Avangard: Problemy, reprezentatsii, i interpretatsii* (St. Petersburg: Palace Editions, 2001), 13–22. In addition, a plethora of documents relating to the State Institute of Artistic Culture have been published in Vakar et al., *Malevich o sebe.*

2. RGALI, f. 665, op. 1, d. 9, l. 83.

3. RGALI, f. 665, op. 1, d. 5, 1. 9.

4. A single document summarizes the activities of the museum between April and October 1921: "Svedenie o deiatel'nost' Muzeiia Khudozhestvennoi kul'tury s 1-ogo aprelia po 1-e oktiabria 1921 goda" (Central State Archive of Literature and Art St. Petersburg [TsGALI SPB], f. 244, op. 1. d. 13, l. 4).

5. Central State Archive St. Petersburg [TsGA SPB], f. 2555, op. 1, d. 374, ll. 19–21. The collection of the Petrograd Museum of Artistic Culture is beautifully reproduced in Basner, *Muzei v Muzee: Russkii avangard iz kollektsii Muzeia khudozhestvennoĭ kul'tury v sobranii Gosudarstvennogo russkogo muzeia.*

6. In 1921, for example, the Petrograd Museum of Artistic Culture was promised ten million rubles for acquisitions and four million for exhibitions and catalog publication (TsGA SPB, f. 2555, op. 1, d. 374, ll. 2–3). Due to the implementation of the New Economic Policy, the corresponding currency revaluation, and the budgetary cuts, it is unlikely the museum received these funds.

7. Zhadova, *Tatlin,* 242.

8. "Otkrytie Muzeia khudozhestvennoi kul'tury," *Zhizn' iskusstva* 28–30 (December 1920): 3.

9. RGALI, f. 665, op. 1, d. 19, l. 43.

10. Al'tman then moved to Moscow and began working in the theater and exhibiting widely at major exhibitions in the Soviet Union and abroad.

11. Andrii Taran studied in Paris in 1909–12.

12. Irina Karasik, "Petrogradskii muzei Khudozhestvennoiu kul'tury," in Basner, *Muzei v Muzee,* 11.

13. TsGALI SPB, f. 244, op. 1, d. 13, ll. 3–3ob.

14. Painter and art critic Vladimir Alekseevich Denisov played an active role in the post–1917 life of Petrograd, teaching at the Higher Art and Technical Institute (VKhUTEIN) and administering the Petrograd Museum of Artistic Culture. He exhibited in 1917 with the "Union of Youth" alongside Tatlin, Karev (also affiliated with the Museum of Artistic Culture), and Al'tman (Basner, *Muzei v Muzee,* 90).

15. Nikolai Fedorovich Lapshin (1888–1942) was a painter, graphic artist, and theater decorator who exhibited with the "Target" group in 1913, was the associate director of the Museum of Artistic Culture in 1921 and 1922, and exhibited in Tatlin's "New Tendencies in Art" in 1922 (ibid., 134).

16. TsGALI SPB, f. 244, op. 1, d. 6, l. 1.

17. Ibid. The Academy of the History of Material Culture was devoted to the Marxist interpretation of world material culture. The Institute of the History of Art, founded in 1912, adapted its programs to a Marxist imperative after 1917.

18. TsGA SPB, f. 2555, op. 1, d. 371, l. 1.

19. Because of the length of the document, I will reproduce small sections here.

20. TsGALI SPB, f. 244, op. 1, d. 13, ll. 7–10.

21. TsGA SPB, f. 2555, op. 1, d. 284, l. 28.

22. GARF, f. A-2307, op. 3, d. 209, ll. 11–12.

23. For example, the Museum of Artistic Culture was instructed to "send all material relating to activities of your institute (protocols, meetings, theses, lectures) regularly to the art department" of Glavnauka (TsGA SPB, f. 2555, op. 1, d. 284, l. 52).

24. TsGALI SPB, f. 244, op. 1, d. 6, l. 5.

25. TsGALI SPB, f. 244, op. 1, d. 9, l. 6.

26. Zhadova, *Tatlin,* 350.

27. Matiushin also brought his students Boris, Maria, and Ksenia Ender.

28. Pamela Kachurin, "Working (for) the State: Vladimir Tatlin and the Origins of the *Monument to the IIIrd International,*" *Modernism/Modernity* 19, no. 1 (January 2012): 19–41.

29. Zhadova, *Tatlin,* 241–42.

30. Vladimir Tatlin, "Programme for the Exhibition 'A Survey of New Tendencies in Art,'" in Zhadova, *Tatlin,* 241–42.

31. Ibid., 242–43.

32. TsGALI SPB, f. 244, op. 1, d. 6, l. 48.

33. For a full list of participants, and a detailed discussion of this exhibition, see O. Shikhereva, "K istorii 'Ob'edineniia novykh techenii v iskusstva,'" in *Russki avangard: Problemy, representatsii i interpretatsii* (St. Petersburg: State Russian Museum, 2001), 53–69.

34. A. V. Lunacharsky, "Sovietskoe gosudarstvo i iskusstvo," *Izvestiia VTsIK* 40 (March 1922): 6.

35. This pro-revolutionary stance may explain why, in the words of Nikolai Lapshin, an artist who participated in and wrote a review of this exhibition, a "Survey of New Trends in Art," was actually "a look at the work and trends of groups united under the name 'leftists.'" N. Lapshin, "Obzor novykh techenii iskusstva," *Zhizn' iskusstva* (July 11, 1922): 27.

36. TsGA SPB, f. 2555, op. 1, d. 475, l. 12.

37. Stuart Finkel, "Purging the Public Intellectual: The 1922 Expulsions from Soviet Russia," *Russian Review* 62 (October 2003): 589–613.

38. Loren Graham, "The Formation of Soviet Research Institutes," in *Russian and Slavic History,* ed. Don Rowney and G. Orchard (Columbus, Ohio: Slavica, 1977), 66.

39. For details, see Irina Karasik, "Petrogradskii muzei khudozhestvennoi kul'tury," in Basner, *Muzei v muzee,* 12.

40. TsGA SPB, f. 2555, op. 1, d. 371, l. 5.

41. TsGA SPB, f. 2555, op. 1, d. 371, l. 5.

42. TsGALI SPB, f. 244. op. 1, d. 6, l. 63.

43. For a detailed description of *Zangezi,* see John Milner, *Vladimir Tatlin and the Russian Avant-Garde* (New Haven, Conn.: Yale University Press, 1983), 199 and following.

44. V. Tatlin, "O Zangezi," *Zhizn' iskusstva* (May 8, 1923): 15.

45. TsGA SPB, f. 2555, op. 1, d. 475, l. 24.

46. TsGALI SPB, f. 36, op. 1, d. 138, l. 3.

47. TsGA SPB, f. 2555, op. 1, d. 5, l. 47.

48. S. Isakov, "Tsentral'nie Muzei," *Zhizn' iskusstva* 13 (April 2, 1923): 7–8.

49. N. Punin, "Komu oni meshaiut," *Zhizn' iskusstva* 19 (May 1923): 15.

50. TsGA SPB, f. 2555, op. 1, d. 475, l. 49.

51. TsGALI SPB, f. 244, op. 1, d. 18, l. 7.
52. TsGALI SPB, f. 244, op. 1, d. 18, l. 11.
53. TsGA SPB, f. 2555, op. 1, d. 647, l. 182.
54. TsGALI SPB, f. 244, op. 1, d. 15, l. 95. He did receive ten easels from the academy.
55. TsGALI SPB, f. 244, op. 1, d. 15, ll. 100–102.
56. TsGALI SPB, f. 244, op. 1, d. 21, ll. 2–6.
57. TsGALI SPB, f. 244, op. 1, d. 21, ll. 2–6.
58. *Narodnoe prosveshchenie,* July 8, 1922, 6.
59. Vakar et al., *Malevich o sebe,* 473.
60. RGALI, f. 941, op. 3, d. 10, ll. 1–4.
61. TsGALI SPB, f. 244, op. 1, d. 18, l. 28.
62. RGALI, f. 941, op. 3, d. 10, ll. 1–4.
63. TsGALI SPB, f. 244, op.1, d. 18, l. 21.
64. GARF, f. A-2306, op. 1, d. 620, ll. 15–15ob.
65. TsGALI SPB, f. 244, op. 1, d.18, ll. 21–23ob.
66. N. Misler, "A Citadel of Idealism: RAKhN as Soviet Anomaly," *Eksperiment* 3 (1997): 14–30.
67. The Central Committee's pronouncement on literature was published in all Soviet newspapers on July 1, 1925. The city of Petrograd was renamed Leningrad in 1924, to honor Vladimir Lenin.
68. Robert Pel'she, "O edinoi khudozhestvennoi politike," *Sovetskoe iskusstvo* 1 (April 1925): 10–11.
69. RGALI, f. 645, op. 1, d. 28, ll. 151–53.
70. As Charlotte Douglas has noted, Malevich frequently employed medical metaphors to describe activities of the research departments. For example, he called himself "doctor" and his students "patients" whose paintings underwent "diagnosis." Charlotte Douglas, "Biographical Outline," in *Malevich: Artist and Theoretician* (Paris: Flammarion, 1991), 16.
71. TsGALI SPB, f. 244, op. 1, d. 21, l. 39. It is perhaps not a coincidence that Malevich's vow to establish a "scientifically precise" explanation of every painterly system—the grandiose goal of his additional element project—was made in 1923, but the project was not completed until late 1924 (TsGALI SPB, f. 244, op. 1, d. 32, ll. 7–8ob).
72. TsGALI SPB, f. 244, op. 1, d. 21, l. 62.
73. TsGA SPB, f. 2555, op. 1, d. 647, ll. 159–60.
74. TsGA SPB, f. 2555, op. 1, d. 647, ll. 298–99.
75. See Karasik, "Petrogradskii Muzei khudozhestvennoi kul'tury," in Basner, *Muzei v muzee,* 19, 21, 23.
76. See, for example, Malevich's June 1924 letter to El Lissitzky, in Vakar et al., *Malevich o sebe,* 1:158.
77. GARF, A-2307, op. 7, d. 11, l. 111. Also see Galina Demosfenova, "Dvevnik formal'no-teoreticheskogo otdela GINKhUKa," *Sovetskoe iskusstvoznanie* 27 (Moscow: Sovietskii khudozhnik, 1991), 472–86.
78. Tatlin remained at the State Institute of Artistic Culture until spring of 1925, at which point he departed for Kiev.
79. Letter from Malevich to Punin, April 23, 1925, published in *Pis'ma Kazimira Malevicha El' Lissitzkomy i Nikolaiu Puninu* (Moscow: RA, 2000), 32.

80. GARF, A-2307, op. 7, d. 11, ll. 34–34ob.

81. GARF, A-2307, op. 7, d. 11, ll. 94–95.

82. Vakar et al., *Malevich o sebe,* 1:175.

83. V. N. Kasatkin, ed., *Osnovye uzakoneniia i rasporiazheniia po narodnomu prosveshcheniiu* (Moscow: Nar. komissariat prosveshcheniia RSFSR, Gosudarestevennoe izdatel'stvo, 1929).

84. TsGALI SPB, f. 244, op. 1, d. 30, ll. 32–34.

85. TsGALI SPB, f. 244, op. 1, d. 30, l. 2.

86. TsGALI SPB, f. 244, op. 1, d. 56, ll. 66–67.

87. P. Novitsky, "Khudozhestvennyi otdel Glavnauki," in *Pervaia otchetnaia vystavka Glavnauki Narkomprosa* (Moscow: Narkompros, 1925), 39–66.

88. For further reading on the theory of the additional element, see Linda Boersma, "On Art, Art Analysis and Art Education: The Theoretical Charts of Kazimir Malevich," in *Kazimir Malevich 1878–1935* (Amsterdam: Stedelijk Museum, 1989); and Mark Cheetham, *Abstract Art Against Autonomy: Infection, Resistance, and Cure Since the 60s* (Cambridge: Cambridge University Press, 2006), 4–5.

89. TsGALI SPB, f. 244, op. 1, d. 70, ll. 9–11.

90. TsGALI SPB, f. 244, op. 1, d. 70, l. 41.

91. TsGALI SPB, f. 244, op. 1, d. 70, l. 58.

92. Employees of the Decorative Arts Institute designed sets and costumes for theatrical productions, textiles, porcelain, and graphic arts.

93. "O dekorativnom Institute," published in Vakar et al., *Malevich o sebe,* 1:518 and following.

94. TsGALI SPB, f. 244, op. 1, d. 50, l. 17. The circumstances around the transfer of the works of art are unclear at best. For more details, see Karasik, "Petrogradskii Muzei khudozhestvennoi kul'tury."

95. *Atheist at the Workbench,* published by the League of the Militant Godless, was a monthly satirical magazine that ridiculed all religious beliefs. For more on *Atheist at the Workbench,* see Robert Weinberg, "Demonizing Judaism During the Soviet 1920s," *Slavic Review* 67 (November 2008): 120–53.

96. Douglas, "Biographical Outline," 18. This politically motivated attack on Malevich's "monastery" can be said to have acknowledged the existence of a functioning family circle in the language of Soviet anticlericalism.

97. Douglas, "Biographical Outline," 18.

98. Vakar et al., *Malevich o sebe,* 2:306. Interview with Konstantin Ivanovich Rozhdestvenskii, one of Malevich's students at the State Institute of Artistic Culture.

99. TsGALI SPB, f. 244, op. 1, d. 50, l. 19.

100. TsGALI SPB, f. 244, op. 1, d. 50, l. 23.

101. TsGALI SPB, f. 244, op. 1, d. 50, l. 20.

102. TsGALI SPB, f. 244, op. 1, d. 50, l. 18.

103. Letter from Malevich to Punin, July 28, 1926, published in Vakar et al., *Malevich o sebe,* 1:177–78.

104. Letter from Vera Ermolaeva to Mikhail Larionov, July 17, 1926, in Karasik, ed., *V Kruge Malevicha,* 130–31.

105. Letter from Malevich to Punin, July 28, 1926, published in Vakar et al., *Malevich o sebe,* 1:177–78.

106. TsGALI SPB, f. 244, op. 1, d. 48, l. 51.

107. Alec Nove, *The Soviet Economic System* (Boston: Allen and Unwin, 1986), 142.

108. Some documents relating to the State Institute of Artistic Culture's activities during this period are published in Vakar et al., *Malevich o sebe,* vol. 1.

109. TsGALI SPB, f. 244, op. 1, d. 70, l. 2.

110. Malevich began his work under the aegis of the State Institute of the History of Art in January 1927, although according to reminiscences, Malevich did not actually move into the building of the State Institute of the History of Art until 1928 or later. See Vakar et al., *Malevich o sebe,* 1:524.

111. TsGALI SPB, f. 244, op. 1, d. 70, ll. 3–4.

Epilogue

1. I. P. Kizin, *Aleksei Ivanovich Sviderskii: Istoriko-revoliutsionnyi ocherk* (Ufa, U.S.S.R.: Bashkirskoe knizhnoe izd-vo, 1971). Glaviskusstvo (Main Arts Administration), which operated from late 1927 to 1931, oversaw all fine arts activities. It took over the functions of the art departments of the Main Scientific Administration, the Main Political Education Administration, and the entire Main Theatrical Administration, thus fulfilling Narkompros's vision of a centralized arts apparatus. The administration of the fine arts was taken up by members of proletarian groups and the Association of Artists of Revolutionary Russia. See Sheila Fitzpatrick, "The Emergence of Glaviskusstvo," *Soviet Studies* 2 (October 1971): 236–53.

2. RGALI, f. 645, op. 1, d. 411, ll. 65–67.

3. The Association of Artists of Revolutionary Russia was founded in 1922. Their platform was one of adherence to the reality of the working men and women of Soviet Russia. See "Platform," in John Bowlt, *Russian Art of the Avant-Garde: Theory and Criticism* (New York: Thames and Hudson, 1988), 265–72. AKhRR was heavily patronized by the state by 1929, and their art is seen as a precursor to Socialist Realism as formulated in 1934.

4. Even the State Academy of Artistic Research (GAKhN), the paragon of state-sponsored intellectual activity, was censured in the late 1920s for disregarding Marxist approaches and was closed in 1930. Sergei Strekopytov, "RAKhN as a State Research Institution" *Eksperiment* 3 (1997): 50–60.

5. Irina Vakar, "Vystavka K. S. Malevicha 1929 goda v Tretyakovskoi Galerii," in *Russkii Avangard: Problemy, reprezentatsii, i interpretatsii,* ed. Irina Karasik and Joseph Kiblitsky (St. Petersburg: Palace Editions, 2001), 121.

6. This cycle of paintings has been the subject of debate within Malevich scholarship. Some have argued that Malevich's depiction of peasants during the onset of rapid industrialization and collectivization campaigns was a concession to the demands for images of contemporary Soviet life, as formulated by the Association of Artists of Revolutionary Russia, while others have claimed that these paintings represent Malevich's last stand as a modernist painter. The other central question about the late figural paintings is their dates. For a fascinating perspective on the question of Malevich's dating strategies, see Charlotte Douglas's argument in "Malevich and De Chirico," in *Rethinking Malevich: Proceedings of a Conference in Celebration of the 125th Anniversary of Kazimir Malevich's Birth,* ed. Charlotte Douglas and Christina Lodder (London: Pindar, 2007), 254–93.

7. Vakar, "Vystavka K. S. Malevicha 1929 goda v Tretyakovskoi Galerii," 134.

8. Charlotte Douglas convincingly argues that De Chirico was an "unseen partner" in the entire late phase of Malevich's paintings, up until 1933, and that although the

works "refer to an earthly prison" they also point to "redemption and ultimate release of suffering—the promise of life on a higher non-material plane" ("Malevich and De Chirico," 285–86).

9. Vakar, "Vystavka K. S. Malevicha 1929 goda v Tretyakovskoi Galerii," 29.

10. For comparisons between Soviet and Western European art production and practices, see Christina Lodder, "The VKhUTEMAS and the Bauhaus," in *The Avant-Garde Frontier: Russia Meets the West 1910–1930,* ed. Gail Harrison Roman and Virginia Hagelstein Marquardt (Gainesville: University Press of Florida, 1992), 196–240; and Éva Forgács, "Malevich and Western Modernism," in *Rethinking Malevich: Proceedings of a Conference in Celebration of the 125th Anniversary of Kazimir Malevich's Birth,* ed. Charlotte Douglas and Christina Lodder (London: Pindar, 2007), 237–53.

11. For more on political culture within institutions in the Soviet Union, see Steven Lee Solnick, *Stealing the State: Control and Collapse in Soviet Institutions* (Cambridge, Mass.: Harvard University Press, 1998).

12. See Marc Simpson, *Uncanny Spectacle: The Public Career of the Young John Singer Sargent* (New Haven, Conn.: Yale University Press, 1997). See also Michael Fitzgerald, *Making Modernism: Picasso and the Creation of the Market for Twentieth-Century Art* (Berkeley: University of California Press, 1996); and Otto Werckmeister, *The Making of Paul Klee's Career, 1914–1920* (Chicago: University of Chicago Press, 1989).

13. Vakar, "Vystavka K. S. Malevicha 1929 goda v Tretyakovskoi Galerii," 255.

14. Shatskikh, *Vitebsk,* 172.

15. Ibid., 40. Ermolaeva was arrested on December 25, 1934, and sentenced to prison camp for three years. However, it was not her professional association with the modernists, but her family connections that made her vulnerable (her brother had been affiliated with the Social Revolutionary Party). Ermolaeva was resentenced and executed in 1937, at the height of the Great Purges.

16. Drevin died in 1938 while in exile in the Altai region (V. A. Kumenev, *30-e gody v sud'bakh otechestvennoi intelligentsii* [Moscow: Nauka, 1991], 202).

17. Punin was arrested in the late 1930s, but was released upon the intervention of his ex-wife, Anna Akhmatova, who petitioned Stalin directly on Punin's behalf. He was rearrested in 1949, and died in the Vorkuta labor camp in 1953, just months before Stalin's own death. On Akhmatova's own strategic self-fashioning, see Alexander Zholkovskii, "K tekhnologii vlasti v tvorchestve i zhiznetvorchestve Akhmatovoi," in *Lebenskunst, Kunstleben: Zhiznetvorchestvo v russkoi kul'ture XVIII–XX veka,* ed. Schamma Schahadat (Munich: Verlage Otto Sagner, 1998), 193–210.

18. For another perspective on the extent to which members of the Soviet "avant-garde" paved the way for the visual language of totalitarianism, see Boris Groys, *The Total Art of Stalinism: Avant-Garde, Aesthetic Dictatorship, and Beyond* (Princeton, N.J.: Princeton University Press, 1992).

Bibliography

ARCHIVAL SOURCES

Moscow

Gosudarstvennyi arkhiv Rossiiskoi Federatsii (GARF)
f. 130 (Council of People's Commissars), op. 5, d. 635
f. 150 (Council of People's Commissars), op. 5, d. 602
f. 1250 (All Russia Central Executive Committee), op. 1, d. 1, 55
f. A-1565 (Main Administration of Professional Education)
op. 2, d. 181
op. 3, d. 160
op. 9, d. 116, 379, 490
f. A-2306 (People's Commissariat of Enlightenment)
op. 1, d. 459, 620, 1709
op. 3, d. 56
op. 9, d. 32
op. 23, d. 7
op. 69, d. 141, 737
f. A-2307 (Main Administration of Scientific and Scientific-Artistic Institutions)
op. 3, d. 209, 210
op. 4, d. 8, 10, 12, 20
op. 7, d. 11
op. 8, d. 133, 154, 160, 162, 182
op. 9, d. 204
op. 10, d. 176
Rossiiskii gosudarstvennyi arkhiv literatury i iskusstva (RGALI)
f. 645 (Central Arts Administration)
op. 1, d. 4, 28, 411
f. 664 (Museum of Painterly Culture), op. 1, d. 1, 3, 4, 8, 10, 11, 12, 13
f. 665 (Department of Fine Arts, Narkompros), op. 1, d. 2, 3, 5, 7, 9, 12, 19, 20, 27, 28
f. 941 (State Academy of Artistic Research), op. 3, d. 10

St. Petersburg

Tsentral'nyi gosudarstvennyi arkhiv Sankt-Peterburga (TsGA SPb)
f. 143 (People's Commissariat of Enlightenment, Northern Region), op. 4, d. 14
f. 2555 (Leningrad Department of the Main Scientific Administration), op. 1, d. 284, 371, 374, 474, 475, 647

Tsentral'nyi gosudarstvennyi arkhiv literatury i iskusstva Saint Petersburga (TsGALI SPB)
f. 244 (Museum of Artistic Culture and GINKhUK)
op. 1, d. 2, 6, 9, 13, 15, 18, 21, 30, 32, 48, 50, 56, 70
op. 2, d. 13
f. 36 (State Museums), op. 1, d. 138
Gosudarstvenyi Russkii Muzei. Otdel rupokisei (OR GRM)
f. 100, d. 249 (Reminiscences of Sophia Dymshits-Tolstaia)

Vitebsk, Belarus

Gosudarstvennyi arkhiv Vitebskoi oblasti (GAVO)
f. 837 (Regional Administration of Professional Education), op. 1, d. 59
f. 1319 (Main Administration of Professional Education), op. 1, d. 1

PRIMARY SOURCES

Bednota. Moscow: Izdatel'stvo Tsentral'nago komiteta Rossiiskoi kommunisticheskoi partii (bol'shevikov), 1918–31.

Biulleten' Glavprofobra. Glavnyi komitet professional'no-tekhnicheskogo obrazovaniia. Moscow: GosIzdat, 1921–?

Iskusstvo kommuny. Petrograd: Otdel izobrazitel'nykh iskusstv Komissariata narodnogo prosveshcheniia, 1918–19.

Iskusstvo: Zhurnal pod otdela iskusstv i sorabisa. Vitebsk: [s.n.], 1921.

IZO Spravochnik.

Izvestiia Vserossiiskogo tsentral'nogo ispolnitel'nogo komiteta sovetov krest'ianskikh, rabochikh, kazach'ikh i krasnoarmeiskikh deputatov i Moskovskogo Soveta rabochikh i krasnoarmeiskikh deputatov. Moscow: Moskovskii Sovet rabochikh i krasnoarmeiskikh deputatov, 1918–23.

Khudozhestvennaia zhizn'. Biulleten' Khudozhestvennoi sektsii Narodnogo komissariata po prosveshcheniiu. Moscow: Gosudarstvennoe izdatel'stvo, 1919–20.

Narodnoe prosveshchenie: ezhenedelnik Narodnogo komissariata po prosveshcheniiu. Moscow: Komissariat, 1918–22.

Narodnoe prosveshchenie: [voprosy politiki i organizatsii narodnogo prosveshcheniia]. Moscow: Gosudarstennoe izdatel'stvo, 1918–30.

Put' UNOVISA, no. 1 (Vitebsk, 1921).

Struggling Russia. New York: Russian Information Bureau in the United States, 1919–20.

Tvorchestvo: Literatura, iskusstvo, nauka, zhizn'. Moscow: Izdatel'stvo Izvestii Moskovskago sovieta rabochikh i krest'ianskikh deputatov, 1918–22.

UNOVIS Almanac, no. 2 (1921).

Vestnik Otdela izobrazitel'nykh iskusstv N. K. P. Moscow: Otdel IZO Narodnogo komissariata prosveshcheniia, 1917–49.

Zhizn' iskusstva. Petrograd: Izdatel'stvo otdela teatra i zrelishch Komissariata narodnogo prosveshcheniia Soiuza kommun Severnoi oblasti, 1918–29.

SECONDARY SOURCES

Abramsky, C. "Eto bylo v Vitebske." *Iskusstvo* 10 (1964): 69–71.

Amishai-Maisels, Ziva. "Chagall and the Jewish Revival: Center or Periphery?" In *Tradition and Revolution: The Jewish Renaissance in the Russian Avant-Garde, 1912–1928,* edited by Ruth Apter-Gabriel, 71–100. Jerusalem: Israel Museum, 1987.

Antliff, Mark. *Avant-Garde Fascism: The Mobilization of Myth, Art, and Culture in France, 1909–1939.* Durham, N.C.: Duke University Press, 2007.

Bailes, Kendall. *Technology and Society Under Lenin and Stalin: Origins of the Soviet Technical Intelligentsia, 1917–1941.* Princeton, N.J.: Princeton University Press, 1978.

Basner, Elena V., and others. *Muzei v muzee: Russkii avangard iz kollektsii Muzeia khudozhestvennoi kul'tury v sobranii Gosudarstvennogo russkogo muzeia.* St. Petersburg: Gos. Russkii muzei: Palace Editions, 1998.

Bastrakova, M. S. *Stanovlenie sovetskoi sistemy organizatsii nauki 1917–1922.* Moscow: Nauka, 1973.

Bojko, Szymon. "Materials for the Study of the History of GINKhUK (State Institute of Artistic Culture)." In *Kasimir Malewitsch zum 100. Geburtstag: Ausstellung Juni–Juli 1978,* edited by Krystyna Rubinger. 280–83. Cologne: Galerie Gmurzynska, 1978.

Bol'shaia sovetskaia entsiklopediia. 3rd edition. 30 vols. Moscow: "Sovetskaia entsiklopediia," 1969–78.

Bowlt, John, editor and translator. *Russian Art of the Avant-Garde: Theory and Criticism.1902–1934.* Revised and enlarged edition. New York: Thames and Hudson, 1988.

Bruk, I. "Mark Shagal i Aleksandr Romm. K publikatsii pisem M. Shagala k A. Rommu (1910–1915) i vospominanii A. Romma 'Mark Shagal' (1944)." *Iskusstvoznanie* 2 (2003): 569–87.

Burger, Peter. *Theory of the Avant-Garde.* Minneapolis: University of Minnesota Press, 1984.

Clark, Katerina. "The 'Quiet Revolution' in Soviet Intellectual Life." In *Russia in the Era of NEP,* edited by Sheila Fitzpatrick, 210–30. Bloomington: Indiana University Press, 1993.

Clark, T. J. *Farewell to an Idea: Episodes from a History of Modernism.* New Haven, Conn.: Yale University Press, 1999.

Cohen, Aaron. *Imagining the Unimaginable: World War, Modern Art, and the Politics of Public Culture in Russia, 1914–1917.* Lincoln: University of Nebraska Press, 2008.

Cohen, Stephen F. *Bukharin and the Bolshevik Revolution: A Political Biography, 1888–1938.* New York: A. A. Knopf, 1973.

Compton, Susan P. *Chagall.* London: Royal Academy of Arts in association with Weidenfeld and Nicolson, 1985.

Cooke, Catherine. "From Theory into Teaching." *Art & Design* 5, nos. 5–6 (1989): 6–31.

Dabrowski, Magdalena, Leah Dickerman, and Peter Galassi. *Aleksandr Rodchenko,* with essays by Aleksandr Lavrent'ev and Varvara Rodchenko. New York: Museum of Modern Art, 1998.

David-Fox, Michael. "Glavlit, Censorship and the Problem of Party Policy in Cultural Affairs, 1922–28." *Soviet Studies* 44, no. 6 (1992): 1045–68.

Demosfenova, G. "Dvevnik formal'no-teoreticheskogo otdela GINKhUKa." *Sovetskoe iskusstvoznanie* 27 (1991): 472–86.

Douglas, Charlotte. "Biographical Outline." In *Malevich: Artist and Theoretician,* 10–12. New York: Flammarion, 1991.

———. "Malevich and De Chirico." In *Rethinking Malevich: Proceedings of a Conference in Celebration of the 125th Anniversary of Kazimir Malevich's Birth,* edited by Charlotte Douglas and Christina Lodder, 254–93. London: Pindar, 2007.

———. "Terms of Transition: The *First Discussional Exhibition* and the Society of Easel Painters." In *The Great Utopia: The Russian and Soviet Avant-Garde, 1915–1932,* 451–65. New York: Guggenheim Museum, 1992.

Dzhafarova, Svetlana. "The Creation of the Museum of Painterly Culture." In *The Great Utopia: The Russian and Soviet Avant-Garde, 1915–1932,* 474–81. New York: Guggenheim Museum, 1992.

Ershova, E. B. *Istoricheskie sud'by khudozhestvennoi intelligentsii Belorussii 1917–1941.* Moscow: Izdatel'skii tsentr Rossiia molodaia, 1994.

Ėtkind, Mark Grigor'evich, and Natan Isaevich Al'tman. *Natan Al'tman.* Dresden: VEB Verlag der Kunst, 1984.

Evans, Alfred. *Soviet Marxism-Leninism: The Decline of an Ideology.* Westport, Conn.: Praeger, 1993.

Fainsod, Merle. *Smolensk Under Soviet Rule.* Cambridge, Mass.: Harvard University Press, 1958.

Finkel, Stuart. *On the Ideological Front: The Russian Intelligentsia and the Making of the Soviet Public Sphere.* New Haven, Conn.: Yale University Press, 2007.

———. "Purging the Public Intellectual: The 1922 Expulsions from Soviet Russia." *Russian Review* 62 (October 2003): 589–613.

Fitzgerald, Michael. *Making Modernism: Picasso and the Creation of the Market for Twentieth-Century Art.* Berkeley: University of California Press, 1996.

Fitzpatrick, Sheila. *The Commissariat of Enlightenment: Soviet Organization of Education and the Arts Under Lunacharsky, October 1917–1921.* Cambridge: Cambridge University Press, 1970.

———. "The Emergence of Glaviskusstvo." *Soviet Studies* 2 (October 1971): 236–53.

———. *Everyday Stalinism: Ordinary Life in Extraordinary Times: Soviet Russia in the 1930s.* Oxford: Oxford University Press, 1999.

———. "Intelligentsia and Power: Client-Patron Relations in Stalin's Russia." In *Stalinismus vor dem zweiten Weltkrieg: Neue Wege der Forschung,* edited by Manfred Hildermeier, 35–53. Munich: R. Oldenbourg Verlag, 1998.

Forgács, Éva. "How the New Left Invented East European Art." *Centropa* 3 (May 2003): 93–104.

———. "Malevich and Western Modernism." In *Rethinking Malevich: Proceedings of a Conference in Celebration of the 125th Anniversary of Kazimir Malevich's Birth,* edited by Charlotte Douglas and Christina Lodder, 237–53. London: Pindar, 2007.

Galin, S. A. *Istoricheskiĭ opyt kul'turnogo stroitel'stva v pervye gody Sovetskoĭ vlasti, 1917–1925.* Moscow: Vysshaia shkola, 1990.

Gorbunov, V. V. *Razvitye V. I. Leninym marksistkoi teorii kul'tury.* Moscow: Politizdat, 1985.

Gough, Maria. *Artist as Producer: Russian Constructivism in Revolution.* Berkeley: University of California Press, 2005.

———. "Futurist Museology." *Modernism/Modernity* 10, no. 2 (April 2003): 327–48.

Graham, Loren R. "The Formation of Soviet Research Institutes: A Combination of Revolutionary Innovation and International Borrowing." In *Russian and Slavic History*, edited by Don Karl Rowney and G. Edward Orchard, 49–75. Columbus, Ohio: Slavica, 1977.

———. *Science in Russia and the Soviet Union: A Short History*. Cambridge, Mass.: Harvard University Press, 1993.

Gray, Camilla. *The Russian Experiment in Art 1863–1922*. Revised and enlarged by Marian Burleigh-Motley. London: Thames and Hudson, 1986.

Greenblatt, Stephen. *Renaissance Self-Fashioning*. Chicago: University of Chicago Press, 2005.

Guggenheim Museum and others. *The Great Utopia: The Russian and Soviet Avant-Garde, 1915–1932*. New York: Guggenheim Museum, 1992.

Gugnin, Nikolai. "Iz istorii Vitebskoi khudozhestvennoi shkoly." In *Shagalovskii sbornik: Materialy I-V Shagalovskikh dnei v Vitebske (1991–1995)*, edited by David Simanovich, 101–15. Vitebsk: N. A. Pan'kov, 1996.

Halfin, Igal. "The Construction of the Workers' Intelligentsia: 'Proletarianization' of Soviet Universities in the 1920s." 2 vols. Ph.D. diss., Columbia University, 1994.

Hemingway, Andrew. *Artists on the Left: American Artists and the Communist Movement, 1926–1956*. New Haven, Conn.: Yale University Press, 2002.

Hickey, Martha Weitzel. *The Writer in Petrograd and the House of the Arts*. Evanston, Ill.: Northwestern University Press, 2009.

Holquist, Peter. *Making War, Forging Revolution: Russia's Continuum of Crisis, 1914–1921*. Cambridge, Mass.: Harvard University Press, 2002.

Il'ina, G. I. *Kul'turnoe stroitel'stvo v Petrograde: Oktiabr' 1917–1920 gg*. Leningrad: Nauka, 1982.

Izdaniia perioda revoliutsii i grazhdanskoi voiny (1917–1921) v Rossii: Katalog kollektsii, edited by N. A. Zemtsova. Moscow: Gos. publichnaia istoricheskaia biblioteka, Otdel redkikh knig, 1991–94.

Junge, Marc. *Gesellschaft ehemaliger politischer Zwangsarbeiter und Verbannter in der Sowjetunion: Gründung, Entwicklung und Liquidierung (1921–1935)*. Berlin: Akademie Verlag, 2009.

Kachurin, Pamela. "Malevich as Soviet Bureaucrat: GINKhUK and the Survival of the Avant Garde 1921–1926." In *Rethinking Malevich: Proceedings of a Conference in Celebration of the 125th Anniversary of Kazimir Malevich's Birth*, edited by Charlotte Douglas and Christina Lodder, 121–38. London: Pindar, 2007.

———. "One Step Forward, Two Steps Back: The Retreat of the Avant Garde in the Early Soviet Era." Ph.D. diss., Indiana University, 1998.

———. "Purchasing Power: The State as Art Patron in Early Soviet Russia." *Biuletyn historii sztuki* 60, nos. 1–2 (1998): 169–83.

———. "Working (for) the State: Vladimir Tatlin's Career in Early Soviet Russia and the Origins of *The Monument to the Third International*." *Modernism/Modernity* 19, no. 1 (2012): 19–41.

Karasik, Irina. "Muzei khudozhestvennoi kul'tury. Evolutsiia idei." In *Russkii avangard: Problemy reprezentatsii i interpretatsii*, edited by I. Karasik, 13–22. St. Petersburg: Palace Editions, 2001.

———. "Petrogradskii muzei Khudozhestvennoiu kul'tury." In *Muzei v muzee: Russkii avangard iz kollektsii Muzeia khudozhestvennoi kul'tury v sobranii Gosu-*

darstvennogo russkogo muzeia, edited by Elena V. Basner et al., 15–17. St. Petersburg: Palace Editions, 1998.

Kenez, Peter. *The Birth of the Propaganda State: Soviet Methods of Mass Mobilization, 1917–1929.* Cambridge: Cambridge University Press, 1985.

———. *A History of the Soviet Union from the Beginning to the End.* Cambridge: Cambridge University Press, 1999.

Khudozhniki narodov SSSR: Biobibliograficheskii slovar', edited by T. N. Gorina et al. Moscow: Iskusstvo, 1970–95.

Kiaer, Christina. *Imagine No Possessions: The Socialist Objects of Russian Constructivism.* Cambridge, Mass.: MIT Press, 2006.

Kizin, I. P. *Aleksei Ivanovich Sviderskii: Istoriko-revoliutsionnyi ocherk.* Ufa, U.S.S.R.: Bashkirskoe knizhnoe izdatel'stvo, 1971.

Kneen, Peter. *Soviet Scientists and the State: An Examination of the Social and Political Aspects of Science in the USSR.* London: Macmillan in association with the Centre for Russian and East European Studies, University of Birmingham, 1984.

Koenker, Diane P. "Urbanization and Deurbanization in the Russian Revolution and Civil War." In *Party, State, and Society in the Russian Civil War: Explorations in Social History,* edited by Diane P. Koenker, William G. Rosenberg, and Ronald Grigor Suny, 81–104. Bloomington: Indiana University Press, 1989.

Kommunisticheskaia partiia Sovetskogo Soiuza v rezoliutsiiakh i resheniiakh s"ezdov, konferentsii i plenumov TsK, 1898–1953. 7th ed. Moscow: Gosudarstevennoe izdatel'stvo politicheskoi literatury, 1954.

Kotkin, Stephen. *Magnetic Mountain: Stalinism as a Civilization.* Berkeley: University of California Press, 1997.

Kovtun, E. F. "Khudozhnitsa knigi V. M. Ermolaeva." *Iskusstvo knigi* 8 (1975): 68–79.

Kovtun, E. F., M. M. Babanazarova, and E. D. Gazieva. *Avangard, ostanovlennyi na begu.* Leningrad: Izdatel'stvo Avrora, 1989.

KPSS vo glave kul'turnoi revoliutsii SSSR, edited by S. A. Andronov and others. Moscow: Politizdat, 1972.

Lebedeva, Irina, Andrei Sarabyanov, and E. N. Petrova, eds. *Nikolai Suetin, 1897–1954,* translation from the Russian by Kenneth MacInnes. Bad Breisig, Ger.: Palace Editions; Moscow: RA, 2008.

Leighten, Patricia. *Re-Ordering the Universe: Picasso and Anarchism, 1897–1914.* Princeton, N.J.: Princeton University Press, 1989.

Lenin, V. I. *Collected Works.* 45 vols. Moscow: Progress, 1960–70.

———. *Polnoe sobranie sochinenii.* 5th edition. 55 vols. Moscow: Gosudartstvennoe izdatel'stvo politicheskoi literatury, 1958–65.

Lincoln, W. Bruce. *Red Victory: A History of the Russian Civil War.* New York: Simon and Schuster, 1989.

Lissitzky-Kuppers, Sophie. *El Lissitzky: Life, Letters, Texts.* Translated from the German by Helene Aldwinckle and Mary Whittall; introduction by Herbert Read. London: Thames and Hudson, 1980.

Lodder, Christina. "Art of the Commune: Politics and Art in Soviet Journals, 1917–20." *Art Journal* 52 (1993): 24–33.

———. *Russian Constructivism.* New Haven, Conn.: Yale University Press, 1983.

———. "The VKhUTEMAS and the Bauhaus." In *The Avant-Garde Frontier: Russia Meets the West, 1910–1930,* edited by Gail Harrison Roman and Virginia Hagelstein Marquardt, 196–240. Gainesville: University Press of Florida, 1992.

Lukomsky, G. K. *Khudozhnik i revoliutsiia 1917–1922.* Berlin: Izdatel'stvo E. A. Gutnova, 1923.

Lunacharskii, A. V. *Ob izobrazitel'nom iskusstve.* 2 vols. Moscow: Sovetskii khudozhnik, 1967.

Malevich, Kazimir. *O novykh sistemakh v iskusstve, statika i skorost', ustanovlenie.* Vitebsk: Rabota i izdanie arteli khudozhestvennogo truda pri Vitsvomase, 1919.

———. "On New Systems of Art." Translated by Xenia Glowacki-Prus and Arnold McMillin. In *Essays on Art, 1915–1933,* edited by Troels Andersen. 2 vols. London: Rapp and Whiting, 1969.

———. *Ot kubizma i Futurisma k Suprematismu: Novyi zhivopisnyi realizm.* 3rd ed. Moscow: [s.n.], 1916.

Mazaev, A. *Kontseptsiia "Proizvodstvennogo iskusstva" 20-kh godov.* Moscow: Nauka, 1985.

McMeekin, Sean. *History's Greatest Heist: The Looting of Russia by the Bolsheviks.* New Haven, Conn.: Yale University Press, 2009.

Milner, John. *A Dictionary of Russian and Soviet Artists, 1420–1970.* Woodbridge, U.K.: Antique Collector's Club, 1993.

———. *Vladimir Tatlin and the Russian Avant-Garde.* New Haven, Conn.: Yale University Press, 1983.

Misler, N. "A Citadel of Idealism: RAKhN as Soviet Anomaly." *Eksperiment* 3 (1997): 14–30.

Narodnoe prosveshchenie v RSFSR k 1925/1926 uchebnom godu (Otchet Narkomprosa RSFSR za 1924/1925 g). Moscow: Gosudarstvennoe izadatel'stvo, 1926.

Nilsson, Nils. *Art, Society, Revolution: Russia 1917–1921.* Stockholm: Almqvist and Wiksell International, 1979.

Nove, Alec. *The Soviet Economic System.* Boston: Allen and Unwin, 1986.

Novitskii, P. "Khudozhestvennyi otdel Glavnauki." In *Pervaia otchetnaia vystavka Glavnauki Narkomprosa,* 39–66. Moscow: Narkompros, 1925.

O'Connor, Timothy. *The Politics of Soviet Culture: Anatolii Lunacharsky.* Ann Arbor, Mich.: UMI Research Press, 1983.

Osnovnye uzakoneniia i rasporiazheniia po narodnomu prosveshcheniiu, edited by V. N. Kasatkin. Moscow: Narodny komissariat prosveshcheniia RSFSR, Gosudarstvennoe izdatel'stvo, 1929.

Pel'she, Robert. "O edinoi khudozhestvennoi politike." *Sovetskoe iskusstvo* 1 (April 1925): 10–11.

Péteri, György, ed. *Patronage, Personal Networks and the Party-State: Everyday Life in the Cultural Sphere in Communist Russia and East Central Europe.* Trondheim, Nor.: Norwegian University of Science and Technology, Program on East European Cultures and Societies, 2004.

Pethybridge, Roger. *One Step Forward Two Steps Back: Soviet Society and Politics in the New Economic Policy.* Oxford: Clarendon, 1990.

Pipes, Richard. *Russia Under the Bolshevik Regime.* New York: A. A. Knopf, 1993.

Pis'ma Kazimira Malevicha El' Lisitskomu i Nikolaiu Puninu: Pis'ma publikuiutsia vpervyc, edited by Aleksandra Shatskikh. Moscow: Izdatel'stvo Pinakoteka, 2000.

Podlipskii, A. *Mark Shagal: Osnovnye daty zhizni i tvorchestva.* Vitebsk: Dom-muzei Marka Shagala, 1993.

Punin, N. N. *O Tatline.* Moscow: RA, 1994.

Radlov, N. E. *O futurizme.* Petrograd: Akvilon, 1923.

Rakitin, Vasilii. "Malevich und INKhuK." In *Kasimir Malewitsch zum 100. Geburt-*

stag: Ausstellung Juni-Juli 1978, edited by Krystyna Rubinger, 284–98. Cologne: Galerie Gmurzynska, 1978.

Read, Christopher. *Culture and Power in Revolutionary Russia: The Intelligentsia and the Transition from Tsarism to Communism.* New York: St. Martin's, 1990.

Remizova, T. A. *Kul'turno-prosvetitel'naia rabota v RSFSR, 1921–1925 gg.* Moscow: Izdatel'stvo Akademii nauk SSSR, 1962.

Rudenstine, Angelica Zander, editor. *Russian Avant-Garde Art: The George Costakis Collection,* introduction by S. Frederick Starr. New York: Abrams, 1981.

Sarab'ianov, A. D. *Neizvestnyi russkii avangard v muzeiakh i chastnykh sobraniiakh.* Moscow: Sovietskii khudozhnik, 1992.

Shamshur, V. V. *Prazdnestva revoliutsii: Organizatsiia i oformlenie sovetskikh massovykh torzhestv v Belorussii.* Minsk: Nauka i tekhnika, 1989.

Sharp, Jane. *Russian Modernism Between East and West: Natal'ia Goncharova and the Moscow Avant-Garde.* New York: Cambridge University Press, 2006.

Shatskikh, Aleksandra. "Chagall and Malevich in Vitebsk: A History of Their Relations." *AICARC Bulletin* 1–2 (1989): 7–10.

———. "K. Malevich v Vitebske." *Iskusstvo* 2 (1988): 38–43.

———. "Poslednie vitebskiie gody Marka Shagala." In *Shagalovskii sbornik: Materialy I-V Shagalovskikh dnei v Vitebske (1991–1995),* edited by David Simanovich, 245–55. Vitebsk: N. A. Pan'kov, 1996.

———. *Vitebsk: The Life of Art.* Translated by Katherine Foshko Tsan. New Haven, Conn.: Yale University Press, 2007.

Shikhereva, O. "K istorii 'Ob'edineniia novykh techenii v iskusstve.'" In *Russkii avangard: Problemy reprezentatsii i interpretatsii,* edited by I. Karasik, 53–69. St. Petersburg: Palace Editions, 2001.

Sidorov, A. A. *Revoliutsiia i iskusstvo.* Moscow: I. I. Bykova, 1918.

Sidorov, Aleksandr. *P. Vil'iams: Zhivopis': Stsenografiia.* Moscow: Sovietskii khudozhnik, 1980.

Simpson, Marc. *Uncanny Spectacle: The Public Career of the Young John Singer Sargent.* New Haven, Conn.: Yale University Press, 1997.

Smeta dokhodov i raskhodov Narodnogo Kommissariata po prosveshcheniiu RSFSR na vtoroe polugodie (iul'-dekabr' 1919). Moscow, 1919.

Sobranie uzakonenii i rasporiazhenii Rabochego i krest'ianskogo pravitel'stva. Moscow: IUridicheskoe izdatel'stvo R.S.F.S.R., 1917–38.

Solnick, Steven Lee. *Stealing the State: Control and Collapse in Soviet Institutions.* Cambridge, Mass.: Harvard University Press, 1998.

Strekopytov, Sergei. "RAKhN as a State Research Institution." *Eksperiment* 3 (1997): 50–60.

Tait, A. L. *Lunacharsky: Poet of the Revolution (1875–1907).* Birmingham: Department of Russian Language and Literature, University of Birmingham, 1984.

Thomson, Boris. *Lot's Wife and the Venus of Milo: Conflicting Attitudes to the Cultural Heritage in Modern Russia.* Cambridge: Cambridge University Press, 1978.

Tolstoy, Alexei. "Agony of the Russian Intelligentsia." *Struggling Russia.* October 25, 1919.

Triska, Jan. *Soviet Communism: Programs and Rules.* San Francisco: Chandler, 1962.

Vakar, Irina. "Vystavka K. S. Malevicha 1929 goda v Tretyakovskoi Galerii." In *Russkii avangard: Problemy reprezentatsii i interpretatsii,* edited by I. Karasik, 121–37. [St. Petersburg]: Palace Editions, 2001.

Vakar, Irina, and T. N. Mikhienko. *Malevich o sebe, Sovremenniki o Maleviche: Pis'ma, dokumenty, vospominaniia, kritika: V 2-kh tomakh.* Moscow: RA, 2004.

V kruge Malevicha: Soratniki, ucheniki, posledovateli v Rossii 1920–1950-kh, edited by Irina Karasik. [St. Petersburg]: Palace Editions, 2000.

Von Geldern, James. *Bolshevik Festivals: 1917–1920.* Berkeley: University of California Press, 1993.

Vostretsova, Liudmila, Tat'iana Goriacheva, and Antonina Zainchkovskaia. *Vera Ermolaeva, 1893–1937.* St. Petersburg: Palace Editions: Graficart, 2008.

Walker, Barbara. *Maximilian Voloshin and the Russian Literary Circle: Culture and Survival in Revolutionary Times.* Bloomington: Indiana University Press, 2005.

Weinberg, Robert. "Demonizing Judaism During the Soviet 1920s." *Slavic Review* 67 (November 2008): 120–53.

Werckmeister, Otto. *The Making of Paul Klee's Career, 1914–1920.* Chicago: University of Chicago Press, 1989.

Wood, Paul. "The Politics of the Avant-Garde." In *1915–1932,* 1–23. New York: Guggenheim Museum, 1992.

Zainchkovskaia, Antonina. *Vera Ermolaeva, 1893–1937.* Moscow: Galeev Galereia: Skorpion, 2009.

Zhadova, Larissa A. "Gosudarstvennyi institut khudozhestvennoi kul'tury v Leningrade." *Problemy istorii sovetskoi arkhitektury* 4 (1978): 25–28.

———. *Malevich: Suprematism and Revolution in Russian Art 1910–1930.* New York: Thames and Hudson, 1982.

———. *Tatlin.* English translation by Paul Filotas and others; translation revised by Colin Wright. New York: Rizzoli, 1988.

Zholkovskii, Alexander. "K tekhnologii vlasti v tvorchestve i zhiznetvorchestve Akhmatovoi." In *Lebenskunst-Kunstleben: Zhiznetvorchestvo v russkoi kul'ture XVIII-XX veka,* edited by Schamma Schahadat, 193–210. Munich: Verlage Otto Sagner, 1998.

Index